AF531342

SERVICE QUALITY IN COMMERCIAL BANKS

By

Dr. M. Edwin Gnanadhas
M.Com, M.Phil, Ph.D.
Reader of Commerce
Scott Christian College
Nagercoil
(Tamil Nadu)

&

Ms. Fatima Holy Ghost

DISCOVERY PUBLISHING HOUSE PVT. LTD.
NEW DELHI-110 002

Published by:
Tilak Wasan

DISCOVERY PUBLISHING HOUSE PVT. LTD.
4831/24, Ansari Road, Prahlad Street
Darya Ganj, New Delhi-110002 (India)
Phone: +91-11-23279245, 43764432
Fax: +91-11-23253475
E-mail: parul.wasan@gmail.com
info@discoverypublishinggroup.com
web: www.discoverypublishinggroup.com

First Edition: **2011**
ISBN: 978-81-8356-825-8

Service Quality in Commercial Banks

Printed at:
Shree Balaji Art Press
Delhi

Preface

Quality, in service, is very important, especially for the growth and development of service sector business enterprises. In the past, quality was measured only for the tangible products because of less dominance of service sector in the economy. Due to the increasing importance of service sector in the economy, the measurement of service quality has become important. Banking is essentially a high contact service industry and there is close interaction between service provider and the customers in the traditional banking scenario.

Service marketing is different from goods marketing because of the inherent difference in services as compared to goods. The service is intangible, heterogeneous, production and consumption takes place simultaneously and it is perishable. These results show the challenge based on the service business and has given rise to the need for new concepts and approaches for marketing and managing service businesses.

In this book, the service quality is focused at two different dimensions namely Service Quality: The Customers' Mind and Service Quality: Managerial Implementation. Chapter One contains introduction, objectives limitation and tools applied. Chapter Two presents the review of related studies. Chapter Three exhibits the customers profile in commercial banks. Chapter Four reveals the demographic discriminators of service quality in banking industry. Chapter Five deals with customer segmentation analysis and Chapter Six contains the findings, suggestions and policy implications.

This book is primarily indented to serve as a textbook for graduates and Research scholars in all disciplines of various universities. It is hoped that the book shall provide guidelines to all interested in research studies.

We shall feel amply rewarded if the book proves helpful in the development of genuine research studies. We look forward suggestions from all readers, scholars and researchers for further improving the subject content of this book.

We gratefully thank Dr.S.Chellakumar Rose, Principal, Scott Christian College(Autonomous) for his encouragement, support and for being a constant source of inspiration.

Our sincere thanks go to Dr.R.Rathiha, Associate Professor of Commerce, Womens' Christian College, Nagercoil and Dr. X. Antony Thanaraj, Associate Professor of Commerce, Scott Christian College (Autonomous), Nagercoil, for their help and encouragement to complete the work.

It is our bounden duty to thank G. Arul Singh who at every stage of our programme has been our sustenance and stay. To him, we express our overwhelming gratitude. We express our sincere thanks to our friends and relatives for their help. We also thank Discovery Publishing House Private Ltd, New Delhi for publishing this book.

Dr. M.Edwin Gnanadhas

S.Fatima Holy Ghost

Contents

1 Introduction

Indian banking sector is presently in the process of completing one full circle. Initially, it was in private sector and moved to public sector with the nationalisation of banks in two stages in 1969 and 1980. Now, with the proposed move of the Government, to reduce the share of public sector from 51 to 33 per cent, public sector banking is again moving in the direction of partial privatization. At present, the number of banks is 299 out of which scheduled banks are 103 and regional rural banks are 196. The State Banks group consists of 7 banks whereas the nationalised banks are 19 in number. The foreign and private banks are 44 and 33 banks respectively. The number of bank branches are 65908 (Ammannaya, 2004).[1]

Substantial liberalisation of the financial services sector has led to increasingly competitive environment in which the market share of government banks has been reduced. Customers in major urban centers, have not only indented their choices, but also get benefited from competitive prices and improved services. The market has changed drastically and has become largely customer centric. The key to success in this changed competitive environment will be one's ability to reach the Chits at his door step and meet his requirement of product and services in a customized manner, leading to customer delight and customer ecstasy. This will call for innovation in the abilities to identify, anticipate, manage and mitigate risks in the process of adverse selection of customers, not only with the existing products and services but also in relation to the banking products of tomorrow. A critical analysis on strength and weakness of the banks, compared to their competitors is highly needed to provide enriched service quality.

Service Quality and its Applications in the Banking Sector

Zeithaml and Bitner(2000)[2] have identified that customers do not perceive quality as a uni-dimensional concept. Rather their assessment of quality includes perceptions of multiple factors. Bahia and Nantel (2000)[3] have suggested six important dimensions of banking service quality namely effectiveness and assurance, access, price, tangibles, service portfolio and reliability. Johnston (1997)[4] identified eighteen service quality variables in retail banking namely commitment, attentiveness, friendliness, care, courtesy, responsiveness, flexibility, competence, comfort, communication, availability, access, cleanliness, security, reliability, functionality, integrity and aesthetics. Abdullah and Francis (2002)[5] extended the Groonroos (1979)[6] model to measure the service quality of commercial banks. They identified functional and technical service quality. The functional service quality includes accessibility, behaviour of staff, attitude of the management, inter-relationships, customer contact, appearance of staff and service mindedness whereas the technical service quality includes technical solution to customers, knowledge of the management, automation, technical ability of employees and computerized systems.

Niki et al., (2006)[7] identified 31 items of service quality relevant to banking sector. In the Indian context, Sharma and

Mehta (2004)[8] Bhat (2005)[9] and Rahman (2005)[10] used five important service quality dimensions namely tangibles, reliability, responsiveness, assurance and empathy. Elango and Gudep (2006)[11] have identified ten service quality dimensions of Indian Commercial banks namely tangibility, reliability, responsiveness, competence, courtesy, creditability, security, access, communication and understanding the customer. Joshua and Koshi (2005)[12] measured the service quality gap in the Indian Commercial Banks with the help of six service quality dimensions namely tangibility, reliability, responsiveness, assurance, empathy and price. In the present study, the service quality of commercial banks is measured with the help of twenty four variables as used by Gani and Bhat,(2003)[13]. With this conceptional background, the present study has made an attempt for mapping the service quality in the Indian Banking Industry.

Need for the Study

A key problem, facing the banking industry is the determination of a clear and precise definition of quality (Bowan and Hedges, 1993)[14]. Bowan and Hedges stated that most conceptualisations of service quality focus on the means as opposed to the ends. Bailing on this relief, they offered several suggestions for banks seeking to distinguish themselves from the competitors. Among these suggestions are that banks need to understand what service quality is (and what is not), and develop customer focused quality standards. The present study noted that answers to these questions can be obtained by simply asking the basic questions 'What do customers want?" and "What they feel about it".

Bowan and Hedges also advocated the first Manhattan Consulting group's services of steps for achieving service quality. The first step requires "selecting the most important customers to satisfy". More specifically, Bowan and Hedges (1993) noted that the importance of various quality improvements differs among customer segments. It is particularly important to focus first on those customers who are most valuable to the bank. One possible method of determining those valuable customers and their level of expectation and perception on service quality is by utilizing customers' demographics. Hence, the present study focuses on this aspect.

Statement of the Problem

In the globalised era, financial sector reforms have significantly deregulated the markets. The commercial bank is not an exception. There are so many foreign banks and new private sector banks coming into the market. The service providers are adopting so many customer-oriented practices, to attract new customers and to retain the existing customers. Since the customers' base is one of the important factors which determine the profit of the commercial banks, the banks have to concentrate more on customer's segmentation analysis and try to satisfy all groups of customers.

The focus on various groups of customers is not an easy task since their level of expectation and perception on various qualities of banking is different. The unique marketing strategies in banking industry may not fulfill the objectives of the banks to the full. Now the commercial banks are realizing the differentiated marketing strategies which are suitable in different market segments. The hectic problem for the service provider is the analysis on the customer segments. If the customer segmentation analysis is properly and, consistently and scientifically done by the service provider, they can deliver the right service to the right customer at the right time. This is the only possible way to survive in the competitive environment. But it requires a permanent customer cell which will undertake the research and development work in the commercial banks.

Objectives of the Study

The objectives of the present study are summarized below:

1. To exhibit the profile of the customers in selected banks;
2. To identify the service quality factors in commercial banks and customer satisfaction towards the banks;
3. To analyse the level of expectation on service quality in commercial banks;
4. To examine the role of demographic profile variables in the customers' expectation;
5. To evaluate the level of perception on service quality in commercial banks in different customer segments;
6. To analyse the impact of perception on service quality of commercial banks on customers satisfaction and
7. To identify the important discriminate service quality factors in different customer segments.

Methodology

Research methodology is the way of systematically and scientifically solving the research problem. It is a blue print of the way in which the research is going to be conducted. The research methodology enlightens the methods to be followed in research activities, starting from problem identification to presentation of research report. It includes research design, locale of research, sampling framework, sources of data, collection of data, framework of analysis and limitations.

Research Design of the Study

A research design is the overall plan or programme of research. It includes an outline of what the investigator will do from writing the hypotheses and their operational implications to the final analysis of data. The research design of the present study is descriptive in nature.

Since the present study describes the characteristics of the customers in commercial banks, service quality in commercial banks, the level of expectation and perception on service quality factors in commercial banks, the customers' satisfaction towards the banks, the impact of service quality in commercial banks on the customers' satisfaction and also the association between the profile of the customers and their expectation and perception on service quality factors, it is descriptive in nature. Apart from this, as this study is confined to pre-determined objectives and also depends upon pre-planned methodology to fulfill the objectives of the study, it is descriptive in nature.

Locale of Research

While studying the service quality in commercial banks, it is imperative to select bank branches and customers of banks. In the present study, it was decided to include the commercial banks in urban, semi-urban and rural areas of Kanyakumari district.

Selection of the Study Area

The researcher selected Kanyakumari district as the study area for the following reasons:

1. There was no recent exclusive study on the service quality in commercial banks in Kanyakumari district.
2. Kanyakumari district consists of urban, semi-urban and rural areas. Hence, the customers belonging to these areas may reveal their opinions on service quality which are versatile in nature.
3. The researcher is very familiar to the culture, local dialect and infrastructure facilities available in this district. The researcher has a good rapport with the customers, which is highly essential for the response on the questionnaire/schedule.

Number of Bank Branches in Kanyakumari District

The commercial banks in the present study are confined to Public Sector Banks (PSBs), Private Sector Banks (PrSBs) and New Private Sector Banks (NPrSBs). The branches in the district are classified into branches in urban, semi urban and rural areas. The number of PSBs, PrSBs and NPrSBs in the above said three areas are presented in Table No.1.1.

Table 1.1: Number of Bank Branches in Kanyakumari District

Sl. No.	Banks	Number of Branches in			Total
		Urban	Semi Urban	Rural	
1.	Public Sector Banks (PSBs)	33	66	13	112
2.	Private Sector Banks (PrSBs)	6	12	7	25
3.	New Private Sector Banks (NPrSBs)	5	1	–	6
	Total	**44**	**79**	**20**	**143**

Source: Annual Credit Plan during 2007-2008, Kanyakumari District, Tamil Nadu.

The total number of commercial bank branches included in the present study is 143. Out of the 143 branches, 112 branches are PSBs, 25 branches are PrSBs and only 6 banks are NPrSBs. On the whole, a maximum of 79 branches are in semi urban areas whereas 44 branches are in urban areas. The remaining 20 branches are in rural areas. In all three areas, the number of PSBs are identified as higher when compared to the other two groups of banks.

Sampling Procedure

Ten customers from each branch have been selected as samples for the study. Hence the sample size comes to 1430. The applied sampling procedure in the present study is stratified proportionate random sampling. The groups of banks and the areas of the banks are treated as the strata of the present study. The distribution of samples is shown in Table. 1.2.

Table 1.2: Number of Samples Selected for the Study

Sl. No.	Banks	Number of Branches in			Total
		Urban	Semi Urban	Rural	
1.	Public Sector Banks (PSBs)	330	660	130	1120
2.	Private Sector Banks (PrSBs)	60	120	70	250
3.	New Private Sector Banks (NPrSBs)	50	10	–	60
	Total	**440**	**790**	**200**	**1430**

Out of the 1430 samples only 43.56 per cent of the customers responded to the questionnaire. The number of customers in PSBs, PrSBs and NPrSBs with response are 387, 179 and 57 respectively. At the same time, in urban, semi urban and rural areas, the responsive customers are 208, 318 and 97 respectively.

Operationalisation and Measurement of Variables

The variables included in the present study are purely descriptive in nature. Hence, it is imperative to correct the normal scale variables into interval scale variables with the help of sealing techniques. The variables and the measurement procedures followed in the present study are given in detail.

Service Quality

Service quality is considered as a comparison between the customers' expectations and their perceptions of the company's actions (Parasuraman et al., 1985[15]; 1998[16]; Boulding et al., 1993; Groonroos, 1994). Perceived service quality has been defined as the consumer's global attitude or judgement of the overall excellence or superiority of the service. Perceived service quality results from comparisons of consumers' expectations with their perceptions of service delivered by suppliers (Lewis et al., 1994[17]; Takeuchi and Quelch, 1983[18]; Zeithaml, 1988[19]). Customers' expectation are beliefs about a service that serves as standards against which service performance is judged (Zeithaml et al., 1993)[20]; what customers think a service provider should offer rather than what might be on offer (Parasuraman et al., 1988). Expectations are formed from a variety of sources such as the customer's personal needs or wishes (Edvardsson et al., 1994)[21].

Service Quality Dimensions in Commercial Banks

Several researchers have suggested that the search for universal conceptualization of the service quality construct may be futile (Levist, 1981[22]; Lovelock, 1983[23]). The service quality construct is either industry or context specific (Babakus and Boller, 1992). The measurements of the service quality construct are multidimensional. In its original structure, service quality consists of five dimensions (Parasuraman et al., 1988; Carman, 1990[24]; Rust and Oliver, 1994[25]). They are:

1. The tangibility aspects of the service;
2. The reliability of the service provider;
3. The assurance provided by the service provider;
4. The responsiveness of the service provider; and
5. The service providers' empathy with customers.

Customers' Satisfaction

Satisfaction is an affective construct rather than a cognitive construct (Oliver, 1997[26]; Olsen, 2002[27]). Rust and Oliver (1994)[28] further defined satisfaction as the "Customer's fulfillment, response", which is an evaluation as well as an emotion-based response to a service. It is an indication of the customer's relief on the probability of a service, leading to a positive feeling. While Cronin et al., (2000)[29] assessed service satisfaction using items that include interest, enjoyment, surprise, anger, wise choice, and doing the right thing, this paper uses the more popular Westbrook and Oliver's (1991)[30] assessed four emotion-laden items. The items are related to self satisfaction, wise decision, right choice and enjoyment.

Consumer Satisfaction

Several studies are seen to conclude that satisfaction is an affective construct rather than a cognitive construct (Oliver, 1997; Olsen, 2002). Rust and Oliver (1994) further defined satisfaction as the "customer's fulfillment response", which is an evaluation as well as emotion-based response to a service.

A 13-item service satisfaction scale developed by Greenfield and Altkisson (1989)[31] measures service satisfaction related to health care and consists of two predominant dimensions: viz perceived outcomes and practitioner's manner and skills (Nergron- relazemey et al., 1998)[32]. Consumer satisfaction has been operationalized in service satisfaction literature as multiple-item scales anchored at "very unsatisfied/displeased" and "very satisfied/pleased (Donthu and Yoo, 1998[33]; Shemwell et al., 1998[34]. Patterson and Spreng, 1997[35]). In the present study, customer satisfaction has been measured over the 35 SERVQUAL items and another 12 outcome items anchored at highly satisfied and highly dissatisfied on a five-point scale. Respondents also evaluated a single question on overall satisfaction on a five point scale.

SERVQUAL Scale

The SERVQUAL scale is the gap between the perception and expectation on various service quality variables (Churchill and Surprenant, 1982). As there is a gap or difference between customers expectations and perceptions, service quality is viewed as lying along a continuum ranging from 'ideal quality' to 'totally unacceptable quality' with some points along the continuum, representing satisfactory quality. The SERVQUAL scale is measured by

$$SQS_i = \sum_{j=1}^{k} \left(P_{ij} - E_{ij}\right)$$

where

SQS_i – SERVQUAL Scale on Service variable of individual 'i'

P – Perception of individual 'i' with respect to performance of a service firm attribute 'j'

E – Expectation of individual 'i' with respect to a service firm attribute 'j'

K – Number of Service attributes/items

The importance of SERVQUAL scale is evident by its application in a number of empirical studies (Kassim and Bojei, 2002[36]; Witknowski and Woljinbarger, 2002[37]; Jain and Gupta, 2004[38]; Gani and Bhat, 2003[39]; Gouguland Rali Sehgal, 2004[40] and Aggarwal and Gupta, 2003[41]). Some major objections against the scale, relate to use of (P-E) gap scores, length of the questionnaire, predictive power of the instrument, and validity of the five-dimension structure (Shephered and Thorpe, 2000[42]; Teas 1993[43]; Cronin and Taylor, 1992; Bahakus and Boller, 1992[44]).

Peter Churchill and Brown (1993)[45] found different scores being reset with psychometric problems. Validity of SERVQUAL scale framework has also come under attack, due to problems with the conceptualization and measurement of expectation component of the SERVQUAL scale. While perception is definable and measurable in a straight forward manner as the consumer's belief about the service is experienced, expectation is subject to multiple interpretations and as such, has been operationalised differently by different authors (Babakus and Inhofe, 1991[46]; Dabholkar et al., 2000).

As there is vagueness in the expectation concept, some researchers like Bolton and Drew (1991)[47], Brown et al., (1993)[48] stressed the need for developing a methodologically more precise scale. The SERVPERF scale developed by Cronin and Taylor (1992) is one of the important variants of the SERVQUAL scale.

SERVPERF Scale

Cronin and Taylor (1992) provided empirical evidence from industries on using the SERVPERF scale. He used the perception on service quality as a tool for the measurement of service quality. The SERVPERF scale expressed by

$$SQ_i = \sum_{j=1}^{k} P_{ij}$$

where

SQ_i – Perceived Service Quality of individual 'i'

P – Perception of individual 'i' with respect to performance of a service firm attribute 'j'

K – Number of Service attributes/items

The researchers have increasingly started making use of SERVPERF scale to measure service quality (Andaleeb and Basu, 1994[49], Cronin et al., 2000[50]; Brady et al., 2002[51]). The SERVPERF measure has outperformed the SERVQUAL scale (Cronin and Brand, 2002).

Construct Development

The general procedure followed (adopted from Churchill, 1979[52]; Parasuraman et al., 1988) in developing the customer service quality instrument is summarized below:

1. Define construct
2. Identify domain (dimensions)

3. General items on dimensions
4. Collect data
5. Purify instrument
6. Collect fresh data from a new sample, on a set of items, to emerge from the previous step.
7. Further purify instrument and
8. Evaluate reliability, dimensionality and validity of instrument.

The 35 item instrument was customized for the bank and further refinement attempted; findings from a qualitative study, commissioned to establish quality service standards, (Dangar Research Group, 1991)[53] were used in reviewing the suitability of the original SERVQUAL items to the host banks' branches. The instrument was pre-tested at three different stages, namely administering of the questionnaire by fellow researchers, self administering of the questionnaire items by 50 customers, and further qualitative assessment of the questionnaire items by the consultative panel, formed within the host bank and other practioners. The instrument was piloted in 5 each branches at urban and rural areas through exit interviews. A total of 39 completed questionnaires were collected. Suitable modification were made based on the views of the customers and experts selected for pre-test. The final items included to measure service quality and customer satisfaction are presented in Table 1.3. (*See Table on next page*)

Collection of Data

The customers are asked to rate the service quality variables at five point scale, on the basis of their level of expectation and perception. Similarly, their satisfaction towards the banks is also measured at five point scale. All these relevant data are collected with the help of pre determined interview schedule. The customers are motivated to answer all the questions in the interview schedule with the help of the respective bank officials.

Table 1.3: Variables in SQF Factors

Sl. No.	Variables
1	2
I	**Reliability**
V_1	Services as per the promise
V_2	Right at the first time
V_3	Precision in filing system
V_4	Absence of error in service delivery
V_5	Sincere in solving problems
V_6	Precision of account statements
II	**Responsiveness**
V_7	Prompt service
V_8	Communicate what is to be served
V_9	Always willing to help the customers
V_{10}	Respond to the customers' request
V_{11}	Never being too busy to respond to customers' request
III	**Assurance**
V_{12}	Recognition of client
V_{13}	Feeling of security
V_{14}	Knowledgeable employees
V_{15}	Friendliness among employees
V_{16}	Consistently courteous with customers
IV	**Tangibles**
V_{17}	Precision of account statement
V_{18}	Clarity of facilities
V_{19}	Decoration of facilities
V_{20}	Efficacious work environment
V_{21}	Visually appealing equipment
V_{22}	Complementary equipments

(Contd...)

1	2
V	**Access**
V_{23}	Waiting is not too long
V_{24}	Rapidly moving queues
V_{25}	Sufficient number of open tellers
V_{26}	No delays due to bureaucratic factors
VI	**Empathy**
V_{27}	Individual attention
V_{28}	Customers' best interest at heart
V_{29}	Understand customers' specific needs
V_{30}	Operating hours and location convenient to customers
V_{31}	Informative
VII	**Price**
V_{32}	Reasonable fees and commission
V_{33}	Good explanation of service fees
V_{34}	Balance amount which service charges begin
V_{35}	Keeping the customers informed

Framework of Analysis

For analysing the data collected from the customers of commercial banks, relevant statistical tools were used to fulfill the objectives of the study. The statistical tools were selected on the basis of the scale of data and the nature of objectives taken for the study. The applied statistical tools are given below:

1. Exploratory Factor Analysis (EFA)

Exploratory Factor Analysis is an attempt to narrate the variables included for the analysis into factors. Factor analysis is somewhat similar to multiple regression analysis, in that each variable is expressed as a linear combination of underlying factors. The amount of variance, a variable shares with all other variables included in the analysis, is referred to as communality. If the variables are standardized, the factor model may be represented as:

$$X_i = A_{i1}F_1 + A_{i2}F_2 + A_{i3}F_3 + \ldots + A_{im}F_m + V_iU_i$$

where

X_i – i th standardized variable

A_{ij} – Standardized multiple regression coefficient of variable 'i' on common factor 'j'

F – Common factor

V_i – Standardized regression coefficient of variable 'i' on unique factor 'i'

U_i – The unique factor variable 'i'

M – Number of common factors

The unique factors are uncorrelated with each other and with the common factors. The common factors themselves can be expressed as linear combinations of the observed variables.

$$F_i = W_{i1}X_1 + W_{i2}X_2 + \ldots\ldots + W_{ik}X_k$$

where

F_i – Estimate of the 'i'th factor

Wi – Weight or factor score coefficient

K – Number of variables

In the presented study, EFA have been executed to narrate the service quality factors and also degree of satisfaction among the customers.

2. Confirmatory Factor Analysis (CFA)

The reliability and validity of the variables in each factor, identified by EFA, have been tested with the help of Confirmatory Factor Analysis. CFA is used to measure the congruent and discriminate validity. The congruent validity is related to high association between the new construct and other similar constructs. Discriminate validity is related to the distinction of the construct from other unrelated measure. The congruent validity is measured with the help of standardized factor loadings and its significance by 't' statistics whereas the discriminate validity is confirmed by the inter correlation between the factors extracted by EFA. The composite reliability is measured for internal consistency. It is confirmed with the suggested threshold of 0.70 (Fornell and Lancher,1981[54]; Anderson and Gerbing 1988[55]; Ahire et al., 1996[56]; Haider and Supriya, 2008[57]). In the present study, the CFA have been administered to test the validity and reliability of the measures.

3. Two Group Discriminate Analysis

Discriminate Analysis is a technique for analyzing data when the criterion or dependent variable is categorical and the predictor or independent variables are interval in nature. When the criterion variable has two categories, the technique is known as two group discriminate analysis. The unstandardised procedure has been followed to establish the discriminate function: The function is:

$$Z = a+b_1+X_1+b_2X_2+\ldots+b_nX_n$$

where

Z – Discriminate criterion

$X_1,X_2\ldots X_n$ – Discriminate variables

$b_1,b_2\ldots b_n$ – Discriminate coefficients

The Wilk's Lambda was calculated as a multi-variant measure of group difference over discriminating variables. The relative discriminating power of the variable was calculated by:

$$I_j = K_j\left(\bar{X}_{j1} - \bar{X}_{J2}\right)$$

where

I^j – The important value of the jth variable

K_j – Unstandardized discriminate coefficient for the jth variable

$\bar{X}_{jk}$ – Mean of the jth variable for k^{th} group

The relative importance of the variable R_j is given by

$$R = \frac{I_j}{\sum_{i=1}^{n} I_j}$$

In the present study, the discriminate service quality factors regarding the expectation and perception among the two groups of customers have been examined with the help of two group discriminate function.

4. Multiple Discriminate Analysis

When three or more categories are involved in the discriminate analysis, the technique is referred to as multiple discriminate analysis. In multiple discriminate analysis, if there are 'G' groups, G-1 discriminate function can be estimated if the number of predictors is larger than this quantity. The superiority of the function is determined by its eigen value and canmical correlation. The function has the highest value of eigen value and canmical correlation is treated as superior and is taken for further explanation. The standardized or unstandardized procedure has been followed to establish these functions. By these functions, the discriminate coefficient of the variables can be exhibited. The variable which has the highest discriminate coefficient is treated as the most important discriminate variable among the groups. In the present study, the multiple discriminate analysis has been executed, to identify the important discriminate service quality factors among three or more than three groups of customers, based on their profile.

5. 'T' test

In order to find out the significant difference among the two means in two different samples, the 't' test is applied.

$$t = \frac{\bar{X}_1 - \bar{X}_2}{\dfrac{\sqrt{(n_1 - 1)\sigma s_1^2 + (n_2 - 1)\sigma s_2^2 X}}{n_1 + n_2}\sqrt{\dfrac{1}{n_1} + \dfrac{1}{n_2}}}$$ with degree of

freedom = (n_1+n_2-2)

where

t – t-statistics

$\bar{X}_1$ – Mean of the first sample

$\bar{X}_2$ – Discriminate coefficients

σs_1^2 – Variance in the first sample

σs_2^2 – Variance in the second sample

n_1 – Number of samples in first group

n_2 – Number of samples in second group

In the present study, the 't' test has been administered to find out the significant difference among the two means

6. One-way Analysis of Variance

The one way analysis of variance is applied to find out the significant difference among more than two means belonging to more than two groups. It is applied when the variables are in interval scale. The F-statistics is calculated by:

$$F \text{ ratio} = \frac{\text{Variance between groups}}{\text{Variance within groups}}$$ is calculated and compared with the respective table value of F.

In the present study, the one way analysis of variance has been executed to find out the significant difference among the means belonging to more than two groups.

7. Multiple Regression analysis

The impact of independent variables on dependent variables has been analysed, with the help of multiple regression when both the variables are in interval scale. The Ordinary Least Square (OLS) method has been followed, to establish the multiple regression function. It takes the form of:

$$Y = a+b_1X_1+b_2X_2+....+b_nX_n+e$$

where

y – Dependent variable

$X_1, X_2 ... X_n$ – Independent variables

$b_1, b_2 ... b_n$ – Regression coefficient of independent variables

a – Constant and

e – Error term

The multiple regression analysis has been applied to find out the impact of perception on service quality in commercial banks on customers satisfaction.

8. Index Preparation

The customer satisfaction Index has been generated with the help of an Index as below:

$$I = \frac{\sum_{i=1}^{n} S_i}{\sum_{i=1}^{n} MS_i} \times 100$$

where

S – Score of the variables

MS – Maximum score of the variables

I=1...n – Number of variables included in a particular measurement.

Limitations of the Study

The present study is subjected to the following limitations:

1. The study is confined to the commercial banks in Kanniyakumari District.
2. The variables related to service quality of commercial banks and the customers' satisfaction towards the banks are selected from the reviews and the views of the experts in the banking industry.
3. The sample size is determined by an unscientific way.
4. The level of expectation and perception on service quality is focused only on the service quality factors narrated by factor analysis.
5. The weightage given on service quality factor is equal.
6. Only limited demographic profile of the customers has been included in the study and
7. The linear relationship between the dependent and independent variables is assumed in the application of multiple regression analysis.

Scheme of the Report

For a neat and clear presentation of the report, the report is divided into six chapters.

Chapter-I includes the scenario of banking industry, service quality of banking industry, need for the study, statement of the problem, objectives of the study, methodology, limitations and scheme of the study.

Chapter-II covers the conceptual framework, review of previous studies and research gap.

Chapter-III explains the paleographic profile of the customers, service quality of commercial banks, customer satisfaction and the service quality in various groups of banks.

Chapter-IV examines the level of expectation on service quality of commercial banks among different groups of customers and the discriminate service quality factors among the groups.

Chapter-V consists of the level of perception on service quality of commercial banks, gap between their perception and expectation on service quality, impact of perception on service quality on customer satisfaction and discriminate service quality factors among the different groups of customers, based on their perception.

Chapter-VI contains the summary of findings, conclusions, research implications and managerial implications.

REFERENCES

1. Ammannaya, K.K (2004), "Indian Banking: 2004", *IBA Bulletin*, 26(1), January, p. 158.
2. Zeithaml, V.A and Bitner, M.J (2000), "Services Marketing: Integrating customer focus across the firm, MC.Graw Hill, New York, NY.
3. Kamilia Bahia and Jacques Nantel (2000), "A Reliable and Valid Measurement Scale for the Perceived Service Quality of Banks", *International Journal of Bank Marketing*, 18(2), pp. 84-91.

4. Robert Johnston (1997), "Identifying the Critical Determinants of Service Quality in Retail Banking: Importance and Effect", *International Journal of Bank Marketing*; 15(4), pp. 111-116.

5. Abdulah H. Aladdaigan and Francis A-Buttle (2002), "Systra – SQ: A New Measure of Bank Service Quality", *International Journal of Service Industry Management*, 13(4), pp. 362-381.

6. Groonroos, C (1979): An Applied Theory for Marketing Industrial Services Industrial Marketing Management.

7. Niki Glaveli, Eugenia Petridon, Chris Liassides and Charalambos Spathus (2006), "Bank Service Quality: Evidence from Five Balkan Countries", *Managing Service Quality*, 16(4), pp. 380-394.

8. Alka Sharma and Versha Mehta (2005), "Service Quality Perceptions in Financial Services – A Case Study of Banking Services", *Journal of Services Research*, 4(2), October-March, pp. 205-221.

9. Mushtag A.Bhat (2005), "Service Quality Perceptions in Banks – A Comparative Analysis", *Vision – The Journal of Business Perspectives*, 9(1), January-March, pp. 11-20.

10. Zillur Rahman (2005), "Service Quality: Gaps in the Indian Banking Industry", *The ICFAI Journal of Marketing Management*, February, pp. 37-46.

11. Rengasamy Elango and Vijayakumar Gudep (2006), "A Comparative Study on the Service Quality and Customer Satisfaction Among Private, Public and Foreign Banks",*The ICFAI Journal of Marketing Management*, 5(3), pp. 7-24.

12. Joshua, A.J and Moli. P.Koshi (2005), "Expectations and Perceptions of Service Quality in Old and New Generation Banks – A Study of Selected Banks in the South Canara Region", *Indian Journal of Marketing*, 35(9), September, pp. 6-11.

13. Gani, A and Mushtag, A.Bhat (2003), "Service Quality in Commercial Banks: A Comparative Study", *Paradigm*, 7(1), pp. 24-36.

14. Bowan, J.W and Hedges, R.B (1993), "Increasing Service Quality in Retail Banking", *Journal of Banking*, 15(1), pp 21-28.

15. Parasuraman, A., Zeithaml, V and Berry, L. (1985), "A Conceptional Model of Service Quality and Implications for Future Research", *Journal of Marketing*, Fall (49), pp. 41-50.

16. Parasuraman, A., Zeithaml, V and Berry, L (1988), "SERVQUAL: A Multiple Item Scale for Measuring Consumer Perceptions of Service Quality", *Journal of Retailing Spring* (64), pp. 12-40.

17. Lewis, B.R., Orledge, J and Mitchell, V.W (1994), "Service Quality: Students Assessment of Banks and Building Societies", *International Journal of Bank Marketing*, 12(4), pp. 3-12.

18. Takeuchi, H and Quelch J.A (1983), "Quality is more than making a Good Product", *Harvard Business Review*, July-August, pp. 139-145.

19. Zeithaml, V.A (1988), "Consumer Perceptions of Price, Quality, and Value: A Means End Model and Synthesis of Evidence", *Journal of Marketing*, Vol. 52, July, pp. 2-22.

20. Zeithaml, V.A. Berry, L.L and Parasuraman, A (1993), "The Nature and Determinants of Customer Expectations of Service", *Journal of the Academy of Marketing Science*, 21(1), Winter, pp. 1-12.

21. Edvardsson, B., Thomasson, B and Ovretveit, J (1994), "*Quality of Service*". Barrie Dale, London.

22. Levist, T (1981), "Marketing Intangible Products and Product Intangibles", *Harvard Business Review*, 59(3), pp. 94-102.

23. Lovelock, C.H (1983), "Classifying Services to Gain Strategic Marketing Insights", *Journal of Marketing*, 47(3), pp. 9-20.

24. Carman, J.M (1990), "Consumer Perceptions of Service Quality: An Assessment of the SERVQUAL Dimensions", *Journal of Retailing*, 66(1), pp. 33-55.

25. Rust, R.T and Oliver, R.L (1994), "Service Quality: Insights and Managerial Implications from the Frontier", in Rust, R.T and Oliver, R.L (Eds), *Service Quality: New Directions in Theory and Practice*, Sage Publications, Thousand Oaks, CA, pp. 72-94.

26. Oliver, R.L (1997), *A Behavioural Perspective on the Consumer*, Mc.Graw-Hill, New York, NY.

27. Olsen, S.O (2002), "Comparative Evaluation and the Relationship Between Quality, Satisfaction and Repurchase Loyalty", *Journal of the Academy of Marketing Sciences*, 30(3), pp. 240-249.

28. Rust, R.T and Oliver, R.L (1994), "Service Quality: Insights and Managerial Implications from the Frontier", in Rust, R.T and Oliver, R.L (Eds), *Service Quality: New Directions in Theory and Practice*, Sage Publications, Thousand Oaks, CA, pp. 72-94.

29. Cronin, J.J., Brady, M.K and Hult, T.M (2000), "Assessing the Effects of Quality, Value, Customer Satisfaction on Consumer Behavioural Intentions in Service Environment", *Journal of Retailing*, 76(2), pp. 193-216.

30. Westbrook, R.A and Oliver, R.L (1991), "The Dimensionality of Consumption Emotion Patterns and Consumer Satisfaction", *Journal of Consumer Research*, 18(1), pp. 84-91.

31. Greenfield, T.K and Altkisson, C.C (1989), "Steps Towards a Multifactorial Satisfaction Scale for Primary Care and Mental Health", *Evaluation and Programme Planning*, 12(3), pp. 271-278.

32. Nergron-Relazemey, G; Alegnia, M; Vera, M and Freeman, D.H (1998), "Testing the Service Satisfaction Scale in Puerto Rico", *Evaluation and Programme Planning*, 21(1), pp. 81-92.

33. Donthu, N and Yoo. B (1998), "Cultural Influence on Service Quality Expectations", *Journal of Service Research*, 1(2), pp. 178-186.

34. Shemwell, D.J; Yavas, U and Bilgin, Z (1998), "Customer-Service Provider Relationships: An Empirical Test of a Model of Service Quality, Satisfaction and Relationship-oriented outcomes", *International Journal of Service Industry Management*, 9(2), pp. 155-168.

35. Patterson, P.G and Spreng, R.A (1997), "Modelling the Relationship Between Perceived Value, Satisfaction and Repurchase Intention in a Business-to-Business, Services Context: An Empirical Examination", *International Journal of Service Industry Management*, 8(5), pp. 415-434.

36. Kassim, N.M. and Bojei, J (2002), "Service Quality: Gaps in Telemarketing Industry", *Journal of Business Research*, 55(11), pp: 845-852.

37. Withowski, T.H. and Wolfinbarger, M.F. (2002), "Comparative Service Quality: German and American Rating Across Service Settings", *Journal of Business Research*, 55(11), pp. 875-881.

38. Sanjai K Jain and Garima Gupta (2004), "Measuring Service Quality" SERVQUAL Variables SERVPERF Scales", *Vikalpa*, 29(2), April-June, pp. 25-37.

39. Gani, A and Mushtag, A.Bhat (2003), "Service Quality in Commercial Banks: A Comparative Study", *Paradigm*, 7(1), pp. 24-36.

40. Raptnaja Gogula and Roli Sehgal (2004), "Service Communication Challenges in the Tourism Industry: Gap 4 of Deintegrated Gaps Model of Service Quality, Revisited Through Selected Cases", *The ICFAI Journal of Marketing Management*, November, pp. 23-31.

41. Navdeep Aggarwal and Mohit Gupta (2003), "Multilevel-Multidimensional Model of Banking Service Quality", *Paradigm*, 79(2), July-December, pp. 91-104.

42. Dobholhar, P.A., Shepherd, Dc and Thorpe, D.I (2000), "A Comprehensive Framework for Service Quality: An Investigation of Critical, Conceptual and Measurement Issues Through a Longitudinal Study", *Journal of Retailing*, 76(2), pp. 139-173.

43. Teas, K.R (1993), "Expectation, Performance Evaluation, and Consumer's Perceptions on Quality", *Journal of Marketing*, 57(October), pp. 18-34.

44. Balakus, E and Boller, G.W. (1992), "An Empirical Assessment of the Serqual Scale", *Journal of Business Research*, 24(3), pp. 253-268.

45. Peter, J.P., Chruchill, G.A and Brown, T.J. (1993), "Caution in the use of different scores in consumer research", *Journal of Consumer Research*, 19 (March), pp. 655-662.

46. Babakus, E and Inhofe, M (1991), "The Role of Expectations and Attribute Importance in the Measurement of Service Quality", in Gilly Mc. (ed). Proceedings of the summer Educator's conference, Chicago, IC: *American Marketing Association*, pp. 142-144.

47. Bolhon, R.N. and Drew, J.H (1991), "A Multistage Model of Customers Assessment of Service Quality and Value", *Journal of Consumer Research*, 17 (March), pp. 375-385.

48. Brown, S.W., Chruchill, G.A. and Beter, J.P. (1993), "Improving the Measurement of Service Quality", Journal of Retailing, 69(1), pp. 127-139.

49. Andaleeb, SS and Basu, A.K. (1994), "Technical Complexity and Consumer knowledge as Moderators of Service Quality Evaluation in the Automobile Service Industry", *Journal of Retailing*, 20(4), pp. 367-381.

50. Cronin, J., Brady, M.K and Hult, T.M. (2000), "Assessing the Effects of Quality, Value and Customer Satisfaction on Consumer Behavioural Intentions in Service Environments", *Journal of Retailing*, 76(2), pp. 193-218.

51. Brady, M.K. Cronin, J and Brand, R.R (2002), "Performance - only measurement of service quality: A Replication and Extension", *Journal of Business Research*, 5(1), pp. 17-31.

52. Churchill, G.A, Jr (1979), "A Paradigm for developing better measures of marketing constructs", *Journal of Marketing* 16 (February), pp. 64-73.

53. Dangar Research Group Limited (1991), "*Quality Service Study*", April-May.

54. Fornell, G and Lancher, D.M (1981), "Evaluating Structural Equation Modeling with Unobservable Variables and Measurement Error", *Journal of Marketing Research*, 18(1), pp. 39-50.

55. Anderson, J.C and Gerbing (1988), "Structural Equation Modeling in Practice: A review and recommended two-step approach", *Psychological Bulletin*, 103(3), pp. 411-423.

56. Ahire, S.L., Golhar, D.Y. and Waller, M.A (1996), "Development and Validation of TQM Implementation Constructs", *Decision Sciences*, 27(1), pp. 23-56.

57. Haider Yasmeen and M.V. Supriya (2008), "Organisational Role Stress: Confirmatory Factor Analysis Approach", *Asia-Pacific Business Review*, 4(2), April-June, pp. 29-33.

Conceptual Framework and Review of Literature

Quality, in service, is very important, especially for the growth and development of service sector business enterprises (Powell, 1995).[1] It works, as an antecedent of customer satisfaction (Ruyter and Bloemer 1995).[2] In the past, quality was measured only for the tangible products because of less dominance of service sector in the economy. Due to the increasing importance of service sector in the economy, the measurement of service quality has become important. Banking is essentially a high contact service industry and there is close interaction between service provider and the customers in the traditional banking scenario.

Service marketing is different from goods marketing because of the inherent difference in services as compared to goods. The service is intangible, heterogeneous, production and consumption takes place simultaneously and it is perishable. These results show the challenge based on the service business and has given rise to the need for new concepts and approaches for marketing and managing service businesses.

Quality

ISO standards is one of the measurement tools of service quality, where quality is defined as the totality of features and characteristics of a product, process or service. Crossby (1979),[3] a renowned researcher in service quality, defined quality as the 'conformance to requirements'.

The guru of quality movement, Juran (1992)[4] defined quality as 'fitness for use' while Lewis (2001)[5] viewed quality as a process promising to result in products or services. Parasuraman et.al., (1994)[6] explained quality as a gap between what customers feel should be offered and what is provided.

Service Quality

Quality in services is an elusive concept because of the intangible nature of the service offered and the definition of quality may vary from person to person and from situation to situation. According to Lasser and Winsor (2000)[7] service quality in banking implies consistently anticipating and satisfying the needs and expectations of the customer.

Ramasamy (1996)[8] identified three different sets of measures for service quality that a company should be concerned with namely service performance measures, customer measures and financial measures.

In the present study, the service quality is focused at two different dimensions namely Service Quality: The Customers' Mind and Service Quality: Managerial Implementation.

Service Quality: The Customers Mind

Service quality is, by nature, a subjective concept, which means that understanding how the customer thinks about service quality is essential to effective management. Cronin and Taylor (1992)[9] and Oliver (1993)[10] identified three related concepts to understand the service quality of customers as customer perception, service quality and customer value. An understanding of the concepts of perception, quality and value is necessary for managing service quality effectively.

Customer Satisfaction

Customer satisfaction, with a specific service encounter, depends on pre-existing or contemporary attitudes about service quality. (Anderson and Sullivan, 1993)[11] Customer satisfaction and perceived service quality are positively related to behavioural intentions (Narasimhan and Sen, 1992).[12] Favourable disconfirmation (when performance exceeds expectations) can positively affect satisfaction (Oliver, 1981).[13] Customer satisfaction was measured with the help of consumer comfort in service relationships as stated by Oliver (1980).[14] It was measured with the help of comfortableness with the service provider, relationship with the service provider, trust on the service provider, commitment of the service provider and activeness of the service provider. On the whole twelve variables related to the above said five aspects were included to measure the customer satisfaction towards the services (Bendapudi and Berry (1997)).[15]

In the present study, the same 12 variables are included to measure the customer satisfaction. The customer satisfaction Index has been generated by

$$CSI = \frac{\sum_{i=1}^{n} SCSV_i}{\sum_{i=1}^{n} MSCSV_i} \times 100$$

where

CSI – Customer Satisfaction Index

$SCSV_i$ – Score on Customer Satisfaction on variable

$MSCSV_i$	–	Maximum score on customer satisfaction on variable
i=1…n	–	Variables included in the customer satisfaction

SERVQUAL Scale

The foundation for the SERVQUAL scale is the gap model proposal by Parasuraman, Zeithaml[16] and Berry[17] (1985, 1988). As a gap or difference between customers expectations and perceptions, service quality is viewed as lying along a continuum ranging from 'ideal quality' to 'totally unacceptable quality', with some points along with continuum representing service quality. The SERVQUAL scale (SQS) is measured by

$$SQ_i = \sum_{j=1}^{k} \left(P_{ij} - E_{ij}\right)$$

where

SQ_i	–	Perceived Service Quality of individual 'i'
K	–	Number of attributes/items
P	–	Perception of individual 'i' with respect to performance of a service firm attribute 'j'
E	–	Service quality expectation for attribute 'j' that is the relevant norm for individual 'i'

The application of the scale is evident in a number of empirical studies (Kassim and Bojei, 2002;[18] Carman, 1990, 2000).[19]

In the present study, the SERVQUAL (SQS) score is calculated by:

$$SQS = \sum_{j=1}^{k} \left(P_{ij} - E_{ij}\right)$$

where

SQS – SERVQUAL Score of service quality variables

E_{ij} – Service Quality expectation for variable/factor

P_{ij} – Service Quality perception for variable/factor

j=1...k – No. of variables/factors included in SERVQUAL analysis

The positive SQS indicates the excess of expectation over the perception on service quality of the banking variables whereas the negative SQS indicates the excess of perception over the expectation on service quality of the banking variables.

Review of Previous Studies

Chinedu B Ezirim (2005)[20] identified the key factors accounting for customer's choice of retail banks in Nigeria to be security of environment of banking operation, size and financial strength of the retail bank, speed of service delivery, liquidity and safety of deposits, and accuracy of any efficiency in customers' accounts management. Others include convenience on the part of the customers in terms of ease of transactions, availability of packing space, possibility of transactions during normal and past-normal banking hours.

Clement (2005)[21] found service quality gaps in sixteen dimensions namely management perceptions, service quality strategy, service design and service quality specifications in terms of customers' expectation, service gaps, quality supportive financial function, internal communication, coordination, organisations in the value system, service delivery, external communication, contact personnels' perceptions of customer's expectations, human element, consumer perceptions and service quality evaluation.

Joshuva and Koshi (2005)[22] found that the ICICI has outperformed the other three selected banks namely UTI bank, Corporation bank and Karnataka bank in providing quality service. It is seen that the performance of the new generation banks across all the service quality dimensions are better than those of old generation banks in the region. The total average gap score of new generation banks is comparatively lesser than, the score seen in old generation banks.

Krishnaveni and Divya Prabha (2005)[23] "identified the antecedents of service quality as dedicating resources, quality oriented vision, empowering employees, ascertaining customer needs, providing desired environment, monitoring customer expectations, recognition and service culture and job satisfaction. The consequences of service quality are customer satisfaction, customer loyalty, positive word of mouth communication, customer trust and commitment, customer retention and business performance and profitability.

Milind Sathye (2005)[24] found that the partially privatized banks have continued to show improved performance and efficiency in the years after privatization, especially, in financial and efficiency parameters. Partially privatized banks also seem to be catching up with the banks already in the private sector. No significant performance or efficiency difference was seen in these two cohorts of banks. It reveals that the Indian strategy of gradual privatisation has succeeded.

Mushtag A Bhat (2005)[25] revealed that the Indian banks fall much below the perceptions of their customers on all dimensions of service quality whereas foreign banks are exceeding the perceptions of their customers on tangibility and reliability dimensions of service quality. These banks are closer as regards expectations of their customers, not far away from the perceptions of their customers as far as other dimensions of service quality are concerned. This observation revealed bleak reality, that Indian banks do not meet the expectation of their customers.

Mushtag A. Bhat (2005)[26] identified that the poor service quality among Indian banks is mostly because of deficiency in tangibility and responsiveness. The service quality of Indian banks is perceived different according to the income, age and region of the customers. The banks provide comparatively better quality service to business group customers in comparison to service group customers as they are comparatively small in number with comparatively high level of income as against service group customers. Different education levels, however, do not exhibit greater variation in service quality.

Nazrul Islam and Ezaz Ahmed (2005)[27] found that first expected service quality factor in banks is the performing promises by the employees followed by the personal attention and tangible physical facilities. There is a relationship between the perceived service quality factors and the overall quality of the bank. There are significant differences between the service quality of public and private banks. The differences are found in physical facilities, appearance of bank employees, services, willingness to help the clients, courtesy to the clients and working hours of the bank.

Shajahan (2005)[28] found that the important discriminant variables among the highly dissatisfied, highly satisfied and just satisfied groups in banking are their attitude on account summary, debit card and delivery channel. The two key benefits of the availability of web services and CRM packages are productivity front and customer intimacy.

Sharma and Mehta (2005)[29] compared the service quality perceptions in State Bank of India, Corporation Bank, UTI Bank and J & K bank. They identified that the UTI bank has the highest tangibility in terms of the employees, physical evidence and ambience. The analysis of reliability dimension, places the public sector banks far ahead of the private sector banks. Regarding 'responsiveness' the Corporation Bank is the front-runner among the four banks. The analysis also reveals that the J & K Bank has the lowest service quality perception value, whereas the Corporation Bank has the highest perception.

Sundar and Lakshmanan (2005)[30] stressed the need for customer care management in banks to achieve customer satisfaction. The important ways to establish the customer care are the customer complaints management, knowledge update of bank staff, routine steps in complaint management, customer-help desk, complaint audit, training of employees for attitudinal change, institution of award for zero grievance rank, customer meet, rewarding financial discipline, brain storming session and computerization of banking operations.

Zillur Rahman (2005)[31] compared the expectations and perception on the services offered by commercial banks. In all five aspects of the quality services, the mean of perception is lesser than the mean of expectation. The significant mean difference between the perception and expectation is also noticed. The largest discrepancies are found along the 'reliability' dimension. The Punjab National Bank is the highest performing bank since it holds an advantage over others in the area of perceived tangible, reliability, responsiveness and empathy dimension. In general, there are highly significant differences among the banks regarding different dimensions of service quality.

Chowdhary (2004)[32] opined that the customers' presence is followed by their demands for customization and responses are to be shifted to their requirements by the frontline personnel. Any service to be provided to the customer can be differentiated by the service provider from the rest of the service providers as it possesses some unique selling proposition.

Gustafsson and Johnson (2004)[33] concluded that the statistical estimates of importance identify those attributes that have had the greatest impact on a customers' more recent consumption experiences. Whereas direct ratings capture what is more globally salient to customers and thus important over time. As direct and derived ratings contain somewhat different and complementary information, an implication of our results is that researchers might gainfully employ both measures to operationalize importance as a more latent construct to explain loyalty.

Hasanbanu (2004)[34] revealed that the customers expect speed, courtesy and concern from the banks. The system followed in banks needs a review for simplifying the various forms and proceedings for sanctioning loans. The important expected services in rural banks are courteous service, clean bank premises, prompt service, accuracy and introduction and payment on term deposits.

Israel et al. (2004)[35] used the correspondence analysis to measure service quality in public and private sector banks. They pointed out that the private sector banks need to focus more on reliability, credibility and security aspects, in delivering service to their customers. The public sector banks need to improve on aspects such as tangibility, fairness and treatment and more importantly on accessibility and 'courteous behaviour' of employees towards the customers.

Sachdev and Verma (2004)[36] revealed that in the case of banking the perceived performance is below would be level of performance in four out of five service dimensions. That is, the banking services do not even perform at the adequate level in respect of reliability, responsiveness, assurance and empathy. The standardized Beta co-efficients have provided the following order of importance of service quality dimensions in banking industry namely empathy, tangibility, reliability, assurance and responsiveness.

Sanjay and Garima (2004)[37] found that while the SERVPERF scale is a more convergent and discriminant valid explanation of the service construct, it possesses greater power to explain variations in the overall service quality scores, and is also a more parsimonious data collection instrument. It is SERVQUAL scale which entails superior diagnostic power to pinpoint areas for managerial intervention.

Sivaloganathan (2004)[38] identified that the customer services should be personal and professional. In a nut shell, Indian banking has definitely come a long way, in its ultimate mission of providing customer care. However, with a rapidly increasing customer population and the parallel growth of demand for qualitative, competitive services, a lot still remains to be desired. In fact, banking sector reforms will be meaningless if they do not improve customers' perception of bank services.

Sultan Singh (2004)[39] identified that the level of customer service and satisfaction is determined by branch location and design, variety of services, rates and changes, systems and procedures, delegation and decentralization, mechanization and computerization, competitive efficiency, complaint redressal and very importantly, staff skills, attitudes and responses.

Upinder, et al. (2004)[40] identified the most important service quality factors in private and public sector banks from the customers' and employees' point of view. Competence, tangibility and record maintenance seem to be typical factors of private sector banks, whereas the tangibility, reliability and access seem to be typical factors of public sector banks.

Victor Iglesias (2004)[41] found the significant effect of pre conceptions on perceptions during the service encounter.

Preconceptions about the service category distort customer perceptions of the service encounter. The effect of preconceptions on the dimensions of tangibles and reliability is lower. The attribute-based processes, predominate in evaluating banking, insurance, and financial advisory services. The direct effect may become significant, whereas the mediating role of perceptions varies.

Eminbabakus et al. (2003)[42] examined the conceptualisation of Management Commitment to Service Quality (MCSQ). The best indicator of MCSQ is empowerment, followed by rewards and training. The training, empowerment and rewards jointly affect Service Recovery Performance through the mediating roles of employees job satisfaction and effective organisation commitment. The MCSQ exerts a stronger influence on Service Recovery Performance through effective organisation commitment than through employees' satisfaction.

Bharati Pathak (2003)[43] identified that Housing Development Finance Corporation emerged as a leader in the financial performance of the banks during 1995-96 to 2000-01. Its closest competitor was ICICI bank. The performance of the other three banks namely Industrial Bank, Centurion Bank and UTI Bank, lagged behind them, but it was, by no means, depressing. These banks, obviously, have to focus more on improving parameters like credit quality and cost control for them to emerge as the top performers.

Debasish (2003)[44] had used Rust and Oliver model to study the service quality in banks. The study revealed that the ICICI bank and State Bank of India provide better quality service. However, on the whole the public sector banks have failed to satisfy their customers in five dimensions namely tangibility, reliability, responsiveness, assurance and empathy.

Gani and Bhat (2003)[45] found that service quality of foreign banks is comparatively better than that of Indian banks. The important reasons for such poor service quality in Indian banks, are lagging behind on the front of physical facilities, up-to-date equipments, communication material, neatness of employees, prompt service of employees to customers, willingness of employees to help customers, convenient operating hours, banks' having customer interest at heart and employees who give personal attention.

Hess et al. (2003)[46] identified that customer organisation relationships can help to shield a service organisation from the negative effects of failures on customer satisfaction. The first suffering effect, was as predicted, a direct effect from customers' expectation of relationship continuity to customers service recovery expectations whereas the second suffering effect is attributions of causality.

Madhu Vij (2003)[47] revealed that some of the banks suffered heavily due to the financial crisis in the Indian financial system after these banks came into being. In addition, the indiscriminate lending to corporates by some of the banks, along with bad corporate governance, resulted in huge non-performing assets. A comparative analysis of the three private sector banks shows that HDFC stands as a clear winner, with ICICI at number two.

Mittal, et al. (2003)[48] identified that customer relationship management was found to be significantly positively correlated with customer orientation, communication, customer care and handling complaints. Young employees, as compared to elderly employees were found to be significantly different on customer orientation, communication and CRM. There was no significant difference between executives and non-executives irrespective of banks on CRM and its components.

Navdeep Aggarwal and Gupta (2003)[49] identified the important factors in banking service quality to be service time, interaction with the bank staff, ambience and infrastructure and services and banking channel. The most important variables in the above said banking service quality factors are banking hours, availability of staff, pleasant atmosphere in the bank and net work of banking services.

Olsen and Johnson (2003)[50] explored and found that equity and customer satisfaction play an important role in the customer loyalty for banking services. Perceived equity as the psychological reaction to a firm's value proposition, affects loyalty through satisfaction. Equity is a judgement that bridges the gap between satisfaction and behaviour intensions. It was also found that the type of evaluations that customers make, affect the impact that price and product have no loyalty vis-à-vis the pure service component of a service offering.

Prabhakaran and Satya (2003)[51] identified rate of interest as the important criteria to choose the final service provider. There is a fair degree of association between reliability and responsiveness, reliability and tangibility, empathy and responsiveness, empathy and tangibility and assurance and reliability.

Spake et al. (2003)[52] revealed that comfort was identified as an important construct in the development and maintenance of relationships with retailers and service providers. The comfort was shown to have a significant impact on trust, commitment, satisfaction and active service. The incremental understanding of the traditional satisfaction-trust-commitment paradigm have been identified.

Darshan Parikh (2002)[53] analysed the gap between perceptions and expectations of customers on retail service quality at five dimensions namely physical aspects, reliability, personal interaction, problem solving and policy. The highest average gap between the customers' perceptions and expectations is identified in the problem solving dimension, followed by the area of interest shown in physical aspects dimension. The study also revealed that customers have their own preferences and expectations different from what service providers think.

Sachdev and Verma (2002)[54] indicated that customers do have two expectation levels namely desired and adequate and they differ significantly in banking. The customers' 'desired' expectations are enduring in nature and 'adequate' expectations are much flexible and closer to the level of service performed. The customers consider all the stated dimensions of service quality namely tangibles, reliability, responsiveness, assurance and empathy to be important to them, as both their 'desired' and 'adequate' expectation levels have been found greater. The comparison of performance mean scores with 'would' expectations in respect of the two services provides that bankers need to improve and manage the service quality on all of its stated aspects because even the customers' minimum acceptable level of performance is not being served.

Brady and Joseph (2001)[55] defined the customers' perception of the organisation's technical and functional quality, service product, service delivery and service environment, and found that reliability, responsiveness, empathy, assurance and tangibles are associated with the service experience.

Shahid Mahmood (2001)[56] indicated that service quality is derived mainly from image, a dimension which is closely related to management's capacity to enhance the institutional climate and ambience, directed at serving the needs of its students and to the reputation of the educational institute. Faculty and administrative staff, through their personal attention to students in a professional and caring manner, also influence quality. Other factors such as curricular, physical lay out and access to facilities are also significant quality factors.

Verma and Hema (2001)[57] revealed that the selected commercial banks are considerably market-oriented. The public, private and foreign sector banks significantly differ in their market orientation. The public sector banks are the least market-oriented whereas the foreign banks are the most market-oriented. There is a positive and significant relationship between the market orientation of commercial banks and the customer satisfaction. Comparatively, the public sector banks are slow to respond to the changes in the customers' tastes and preferences.

Agarwal and Bapat (2000)[58] attempted to explain in detail about the phenomenon of impulsive buying in services. Services as it has been found, are to a large extent, different from goods as far as eliciting impulsive usage is concerned. The consumer impulsiveness is strongly and positively correlated with the attitude on tangibility, enjoyment value, simplicity, availability, group use and frequency but strongly and negatively correlated with the attitude on heterogeneity.

Amit and Shainesh (2000)[59] concluded that the inclusion of additional variables, measuring relationship strength in the service quality based customer satisfaction measurement, would enable managers to get a deeper insight into the status of customers' loyalty and related behaviours. The satisfaction was an important factor determining loyalty. But the fact that satisfied customers switch, suggests that satisfaction is a condition that is necessary but not sufficient for loyalty.

Aravindan and Punniyamoorthy (2000)[60] found that the customer satisfaction in banking would be achieved mainly by meeting the objective needs of the customers namely performance, reliability and serviceability features and aesthetic aspects played a supplementary role in bringing satisfaction to the customers.

Hasmukh (2000)[61] in his study on delivering quality services at two commercial co-operative banks in Gujarat identified that the quality of services rendered to the customers, shareholders, employees and the community, at large, is the source of satisfaction to all concerned. As a result, there is considerable progress in terms of deposits, advances, loans and profits. All people connected, prefer these banks due to their prompt, cheap, comfortable and personalised services and seem to be quite happy with their experience.

Nath and Mukherjee (2000)[62] identified the service quality in engineering education to be competence of faculty, reliability, placement facilities, academic infrastructure, support facilities and campus facilities. The study also differentiated the quality of service offered by the state-run and private engineering colleges. The private college authorities properly utilize the resources to improve their service quality in a consistent manner.

Oliver Nerurkar (2000)[63] found that the consumers assigned lower weights to tangibles as compared to reliability, responsiveness and assurance. The weightage given on the service quality of commercial banks is reliability. But in the case of insurance, consumers did not distinguish among the five service dimensions in terms of their importance. In the hotel industry, it was found that consumers assigned to reliability a significantly higher weight than assurance and empathy.

Phatak and Abidi (2000)[64] revealed that the clients perception of quality in banking services are reliability, tangibility, responsiveness, assurance and empathy. The private sector banks are definitely more able to meet the expectations of their clients than the public sector banks. Especially on factors like reliability and empathy, the gap is almost negligible in the case of private sector banks while it is significant in the case of public sector banks. On factors like tangibility and assurance, the private sector banks are again out performing public sector banks.

Rawani and Gupta (2000)[65] found that the customers in banks expect faster turn-around times for banking and demand better services than ever before. Due to difference in market segments covered by public and private sector banks, expectations of their customers are also different. Private sector banks focus on innovation and customer service whereas public sector banks work on social commitment. Banks expect customers to be punctual and customers find it convenient.

Shainesh and Mukul Mathur (2000)[66] identified the service quality factors in railways as ability to provide safe and fast delivery, cost of transportation, encouraging flexibility and bilateralism, attitude of staff and officers, convenient wagon allotment procedure, terminal facilities and providing and sharing information.

Verma and Vohra (2000)[67] revealed the significant pattern of importance of banking service quality features as perceived by the customers. Out of the top five features, as perceived by the respondents, three relate to the SERVQUAL dimension of reliability, and one each to responsiveness and empathy. Moreover, most of the customers do not pay much attention to the tangibles. The important perceived aspects by the customers are punctuality in opening of the bank, accurate record keeping and prompt services.

Xavier and Shainesh (2000)[68] revealed that service plays a key role in determining behavioural intentions, like the intention to repurchase, and increase usuage, the intention to use other offerings, and the intention to recommend the service. The study revealed a positive relationship between service quality and disconfirmation, satisfaction, service value, behavioural intentions and objective price.

Sanjay Kumar (1999)[69] identified the important discriminants of the profitable and non-profitable banks in India to be four important ratios namely earning assets to shareholder's equity, spread to working fund, non-interest expenditure to working fund and operating expenses to total income.

Devlin and Dong (1996)[70] believe that improved service quality also cuts costs because companies have fewer customers to replace, less corrective work to do, fewer inquiries and complaints to handle, and less employee turnover and dissatisfaction to deal with.

Research Gap

The above said previous studies are analyzing the perception on service quality in commercial banks by performance only and the SERVQUAL scale measures. They have identified the gap between the level of perception and expectation on service quality in commercial banks. Some of the studies focused the perception on service quality among the customers in different groups of banks. Few studies reveal the position of public, private and foreign banks regarding the service quality context. Only a few studies are focusing on the role of profile of the customers in their level of perception on service quality of commercial banks. But no study has focused on the level of expectation on service quality and the role of demographic profile of customers in their level of expectation and perception on service quality of commercial banks, especially, in Tamil Nadu and specifically in Kanniyakumari district. Hence, the present study tries to fill up this research gap for some policy implications.

REFERENCES

1. Powell, T.C., (1995), "Total Quality Management as Competitive Advantage: A Review and Empirical Study", *Strategic Management Journal*, 16 (1), pp. 15-37.
2. Ruyter, K.D. and Bloemer, J. (1995), "Integrating Service Quality and Satisfaction: Playing in the Neck or Marketing Opportunity?", *Journal of Customer Satisfaction, Dissatisfaction and Complaining Behaviour*, 8 (2), pp. 44-52.
3. Crossby, P.B., (1979), *Quality is Free: The Art of Making Quality Certain*, McGraw Hill, New York, p. 9.
4. Juran, J., (1968), *Juran on Planning for Quality, American Society for Quality Control*, Milwankee, WI.
5. Lewis, P.E. (2001), "An Extension to the process of Customer Service Quality Evaluation Through Psychology and Empirical Study", *Asia-Pacific Advances in Consumer Research*, 4 (1), pp. 281-287.
6. Parasuraman, A., Zeithaml, V.A., and Beny, L.L., (1994), Alternative Scales of Measuring Service Quality: A Comparative Assessment based on Psychometric and Diagnostic Criteria", *Journal of Retailing*, 70 (3), pp. 201-230.

7. Wallaied M. Lassar and Robert D. Winsor (2000), "Service Quality Perspectives and Satisfaction in Private Banking", *Journal of Services Marketing,* 14 (2-3), p. 244.

8. Ramasamy (1996), "Design and Management of Service Process: Keeping Customers for Life", Addison-Wesley, Reading MA, pp. 362-363.

9. Cronin, J.J. and Taylor, S.A. (1992), "Measuring Service Quality: A re-examination and extension", *Journal of Marketing,* 56 (3), pp. 55-68.

10. Oliver, R.L., (1993), "A Conceptual Model of Service Quality and Service Satisfaction: Compatible goals, different concepts. In T.A. Swartz, D.E. Bowen and S.W.Brown (eds)., *Advances in Services Marketing and Management: Research and Practice,* Greenwich, CT: JAI, Vol. 2, pp. 65-85.

11. Anderson, E.W. and Sullivan, M.W. (1993), "The Antecedents and Consequences of Customer Satisfaction of Firms", *Marketing Science,* 12 (3), pp. 125-143.

12. Narasimhan, C. and Sen, S. (1992), "Measuring Quality Perceptions", *Marketing Letters,* 3 (1), pp. 147-156.

13. Oliver, R.L. (1981), "Measurement and Evaluation of Satisfaction Process in Retail Settings", *Journal of Retailing,* 57 (6), pp. 25-45.

14. Oliver, R.L., (1980), "A Cognitive Model of the Antecedents and Consequences of Satisfaction Decisions", *Journal of Marketing Research,* 17 (3), pp. 460-469.

15. Bendapudi Neeli and Leonard L. Berry (1997), "Customers Motivation for maintaining relationships with service providers", *Journal of Retailing,* 73 (1), pp. 15-37.

16. Parasuraman, A., Zeithaml, V.A., and

Berry, L., (1985), "A Conceptual Model of Service Quality and its Implications for Future Research", *Journal of Marketing,* 49 (Fall), pp. 41-50.

17. Parasuraman, A., Zeithaml, V.A., (1988), "SERVQUAL: A Multiple Item Scale for Measuring Consumer Perceptions of Service Quality", *Journal of Retailing,* 64 (1), pp. 12-40.

18. Kassim, N.M. and Bojei, J., (2002), "Service Quality: Gaps in the Telemarketing Industry", *Journal of Business Research,* 55 (11), pp. 845-852.

19. Carman, J.M., (1990), "Consumer Perceptions of Service Quality: An Assessment of the SERVQUAL Dimensions", *Journal of Retailing,* 66(1), pp. 33-35.

20. Chinedu B Ezirim (2005), "Empirical Investigation of Customer's Choice of Retail Banks in Nigeria", *The ICPAI Journal of Applied Economics,* 4 (5), September, pp. 31-46.

21. Clement (2005), "Service Quality Gap Models: A Re-examination and Extension", *SMART Journal of Business Management Studies*, 1 (2), July-December, pp. 87-93.

22. Joshuva, A.J. and Moli, P. Koshi (2005), "Expectations and Perceptions of Service Quality in Old and New Generation Banks-A Study of Selected Banks in the South Canara Region", *Indian Journal of Marketing*, 35 (9), September, pp. 1-11.

23. Krishnaveni, R. and Divya Prabha, (2005), "Service Quality and Its Linkages with Customer Relationship Management-A Comprehensive View", *Udyog Pragati*, 29 (3), July-September, pp. 15-19.

24. Milind Sathye (2005), "Privatisation, Performance and Efficiency: A Study of Indian Banks", *Vikalpa*, 30 (1), January-March, pp. 7-15.

25. Mushtag A. Bhat, (2005), "Service Quality Perceptions in Banks: A Comparative Analysis", *Vision*, 9 (1), January-March, pp. 11-20.

26. Mushtag A. Bhat (2005), "Correlates of Service Quality in Banks: An Empirical investigation", *Journal of Services Research*, 5 (1), April-September, pp. 77-91.

27. Nazrul Islam and Ezaz Ahmed, (2005), "A measurement of Customers Service Quality of Banks in Dhaka City of Bangladesh", *South Asian Journal of Management*, 12 (3), pp. 37-57.

28. Shajahan, S., (2000), "A Study on the Level of Customers Satisfaction on Various Models of Banking Services in India", *The ICFAI Journal of Bank Management*, 4(1), February, pp. 79-84.

29. Alka Sharma and Versha Mehta (2005), "Service Quality Perceptions in Financial Services-A Case Study of Banking Services", *Journal of Services Research*, 4 (2), October-March, 2005, pp. 205-217.

30. Sundar, K. and Lakshmanan (2005), "Customer Care Management in Banks", *Management Marketers*, 1 (3), September-February, pp. 93-96.

31. Zillur Rahman, (2005), "Service Quality: Gaps in the Indian Banking Industry", *The ICFAI Journal of Marketing Management*, 3 (2), February, pp. 37-45.

32. Chowdhary, Nunit and Bhagawati P. Saraswat (2004), "Service Leadership Study", *Journal of Services Research*, 3 (2), pp. 105-123.

33. Anders Gustafsson and Michael D.Johnson (2004), "Determining Attribute Importance in a Service Satisfaction Model", *Journal of Services Research*, 7 (2), November, pp. 124-141.

34. Hasanbanu, S., (2004), "Customer Service in Rural Banks: An Analytical Study of Attitude of Difficult type of Customers Towards Banking Services", *IBA Bulletin*, 25 (8), August, pp. 21-25.

35. Israel, D., Celement Sudhahar and M.Selvam, (2004), "*Journal of Indian Management*, 1 (4), October-December, pp. 37-49.

36. Sheetal B. Sachdev and Harsh V. Verma, (2004), "Relative Importance of Service Quality Dimensions: A Multi Sectoral Study", *Journal of Services Research*, 4 (1), April-September, pp. 59-80.

37. Sanjay, K. Jain and Garima Gupta, (2004), "Measuring Service Quality: SERVQUAL Variables SERVPERF scales", *Vikalpa*, 29(2), April-June, pp. 25-37.

38. Sivaloganathan, K., (2004), "Relationship Marketing in Banking Service: The Need of the hour", *Udyog Pragati*, 28 (2), April-June, pp. 13-15.

39. Sultan Singh (2004), "An Appraisal of Customers Service of Public Sector Banks", IBA Bulletin, 25 (8), August, pp. 30-33.

40. Upinder Dhar, Santosh Dhar and Abhinav Jain, (2004), "Service with a difference: A Comparative Analysis of Private and Public Sector Banks", *Prestige Journal of Management and Research*, 8 (1 & 2), April-October, pp. 17-29.

41. Victor Iglesias (2004), "Pre-conceptions about Service", *Journal of Service Research*, 7 (1), August, pp. 90-102.

42. Eminbabakus, Ugur Yavas and Osman, Karatepe (2003), "The Effect of Management Commitment to Service Quality on Employees' Affective and Performance Outcomes", *Journal of the academy of Marketing Science*, 31 (3), pp. 272-286.

43. Bharati Pathak (2003), "A Comparison of the Financial Performance of Private Sector Banks", *Finance India*, 17 (4), December, pp. 1345-1356.

44. Debasish Sathya Swaroop (2003), "Service quality in Commercial banks: A Comparative Analysis of Selected banks in Delhi", *Indian Journal of Marketing*, 33 (3), pp. 3-9.

45. Gani, A. and Mushtag, A. Bhat (2003), "Service quality in Commercial banks: A Comparative Study", *Paradigm*, 7 (1), pp. 24-36.

46. Ronald L. Hess, Shankar Ganesan and Naveen M.Klerin, (2003), "Service Failure and Recovery: The Impact of Relationship Factors on Customer Satisfaction", *Journal of Academy of Marketing Science*, 31 (2), pp. 127-145.

47. Madhu Vij (2003), "The New World of Banking", *Journal of Management Research*, 3 (3), December, pp. 13-149.

48. Alok Mittal, Jayant Sonwalkar and Akhilesh K.Mishra, (2003), "An Exploratory Study of CRM Orientation Among Bank Employees", *Indian Journal of Training and Development*, 33 (1-2), January-June, pp. 34-44.

49. Navdeep Aggarwal and Mohit Gupta (2003), "Multi level-Multi Dimensional Model of Banking Service Quality", *Paradigm*, 7 (2), July-December, pp. 91-104.

50. Line Lervik Olsen and Michael D. Johnson (2003), "Service Quality, Satisfaction and Loyalty: Transaction-Specific to Cumulative Evaluations", *Journal of Service Research*, 5 (3), February, pp.184-195.

51. Prabhakáran, S., and Satya, S., (2003), "A Right into Service Attributes in Banking Sector", *Journal Services Research*, X 3(1), April-September, pp. 157-169.

52. Deborah F.Spake, Sharon E.Beathy, Beverly K. Brockman and Tammy Neal Crutchfield (2003), "Consumer Comfort in Service Relationships", *Journal of Services Research*, 5 (4), pp. 316-332.

53. Darshan Parikh, (2002), "Measuring Retail Service Quality: An Empirical Study in a Developing Country", *South Indian Journal of Management*, 12 (2), April-June, pp. 43-57.

54. Sheetal B. Sachdev and Harsh V. Verma (2002), "Customer Expectations and Service Quality Dimensions Consistency", *Journal of Management Research*, 2 (1), April, pp. 43-52.

55. Brady Micahel and Cronin, Joseph, J., (2001), "Some New Thoughts on Conceptualizing Perceived Service Quality: A hierarchical Approach", *Journal of Marketing*, 65 (3), pp. 34-49.

56. Shid Mahmood (2001), "Customer Quality in Education: An Exploratory Study", *Management and Change*, 5 (2), Winter, pp. 309-319.

57. Verma, D.P.S. and Hema Israney, (2001), "Market Orientation in Commercial Banks–A Study of Selected Banks in Delhi", *Vision*, 6 (1), July-December, pp. 7-14.

58. Agarwal, M.C. and Suhud S. Bapat (2000), "Impulse Buying in Services: Status and Research Directions", *Delivering Service Quality*, M.Raghavachari and K.V.Ramani, Mc Millan India Ltd., Delhi, pp. 61-75.

59. Amit Mokerjee and G.Shainesh (2000), "Developing Measures for Service Quality and Relationships Strength Determinants of Customers Loyalty", *Delivering Service Quality*, M.Raghavachari and K.V.Ramani, Mc Millan India Ltd., Delhi, pp.29-35.

60. Aravindan, P. and Punniyamoorthy, (2000), "Service Quality Model to Measure Customer Satisfaction", *Delivering Service Quality*: M.Raghavachari and K.V.Ramani, Mc Millan India Ltd., pp. 104-110.

61. Hasmukh D.Savlani (2000), "Delivering Quality Services at Two Commercial Co-operative Banks in Gujarat", *Delivering Service Quality*: M.Raghavachari and K.V.Ramani, Mc Millan India Ltd., pp. 153-158.

62. Prithviraj Nath and Arinvandan Mukherjee (2000), "Measuring Service Quality in Engineering Education-Applicability of SERVQUAL", *Delivering Service Quality*: M.Raghavachari and K.V.Ramani, Mc Millan India Ltd., pp. 247-252.

63. Olive Nerurkar (2000), "A Preliminary Investigation of SERVQUAL Dimensions in India", *Delivering Service Quality*: M.Raghavachari and K.V.Ramani, Mc Millan India Ltd., pp. 571-580.

64. Yogeshwari Phatak and Naseem Abidi (2000), "Client's Perception on Quality in Banking Services: An Empirical Study", *Delivering Service Quality*: M.Raghavachari and K.V.Ramani, Mc Millan India Ltd., pp. 141-152.

65. Rawani, A.M. and Gupta, M.P. (2000), "It Vs Service Quality in Banks-A Few Learning Issues", *Delivering Service Quality*: M.Raghavachari and K.V.Ramani, Mc Millan India Ltd., pp. 167-172.

66. Shainesh, G. and Mukul Mathur, (2000), "Service quality measurement: The Case of Railway Freight Services", *Vikalpa*, 25 (3), July-September, pp. 15-22.

67. Verma, D.P.S. and Ruchika Vohra, (2000), "Customer Perception of Banking Service Quality–A Study of State Bank of India", *The Journal of Institute of Public Enterprise*, 23 (3 & 4), pp. 46-54.

68. Xavier, M.J. and Shainesh, G., (2000), "Modelling Customer Evaluation of Banking Service – The Antecedents and Consequences of Service Value", *Delivering Service Quality*: M.Raghavachari and K.V.Ramani, Mc Millan India Ltd., Delhi, pp. 78-88.

69. Sanjay Kumar, (1999), "Profitability of Indian Commercial Banks-The Key Discriminators", *Management and Accounting Research*, 1 (4), April-June, pp. 21-31.

70. Devlin, S.J. and Dong, H.K., (1996), "Service Quality from Customers Perspective", Marketing Research, 6 (1), pp. 5-13.

Customers' Profile and Service Quality in Commercial Banks

In the competitive environment of the post liberalization era in which, financial sector reforms have significantly deregulated the markets, it has become imperative to harness the best customer oriented practices and perceptions and to internalize them for providing added value to the customers through the employees. In banking, the quality of customer services holds primary significance, particularly in the context of sustained business growth. Unlike the other industries engaged in the production of tangible goods, banks are unique in the sense that they produce and deliver the service instantaneously at the service delivery points. This has an overwhelming impact on customers' behaviour, which makes customers hypersensitive to the quality of service.

Service quality is a customer determination, based on customers' actual experience with the service, measured against his or her requirement, stated or unstated, optional or subjective, conscious or merely sensed.

The customers' perceive the service quality to be high

if it is perfect on his estimation; therefore, it becomes imperative for service providers to meet or exceed the target of customers' service quality estimations. Those customers' expectation and perception are based on their profile. Hence, it is essential to reveal the demographic profile of the customers. In the present study, the profile of the customers include their age, sex, nativity, level of education, family size, occupation, personal income, family income, banking experience and personality traits.

Age of the Customers

Age of the customers is one of the important profile variables of the customers. It shows their level of experience and maturity. In the banking industry, age plays a predominant role in their level of expectation and perception on the service quality of the commercial banks. In general, the youngsters expect more than the elders who are highly experienced and emotionally balanced. The age of the customers in the present study is confined to less than 25 years, 25-35, 36 to 45, 46 to 55, 56 to 65 and above 65 years. The distribution of customers on the basis of their age is given in Table 3.1.

Table: 3.1: Age-wise Distribution of the Customers

Sl. No.	Age (in years)	Number of Customers in			Total
		PSBs	PrsBS	NPrSBs	
1.	Less than 25	17	29	13	59
2.	25-35	115	32	11	158
3.	36-45	115	27	12	154
4.	46-55	64	33	8	105
5.	56-65	50	41	10	101
6.	Above 65	26	17	3	46
	Total	**387**	**179**	**57**	**623**

From the above table it is clear that the important age groups among the customers is 25 to 35 years and 36 to 45 years which constitute 25.36 and 24.72 per cent to their respective total. The number of customers with the age of above 65 years constitutes 7.38 per cent to the total. The most important age category among the customers of PSBs is 25 to 35 years and 36 to 45 years which constitute 29.72 per cent to their respective total. In the case of Private Sector Banks, these are 56 to 65 years and 46 to 55 years constituting 22.91 and 18.44 per cent to their respective total. Among the customers of NPrSBs, the prominent age groups are less than 25 years and 36 to 45 years which constitute 22.81 and 21.05 per cent to their respective total. The analysis reveals that the important age groups among the customers in the present study are 25 to 35 years and 36 to 45 years.

Gender of the Customers

Since the gender of the customers has its own role in their level of expectation and perception on the service quality of commercial banks, it is included as one of the profile variables. The female customers are usually seeking more service quality from commercial banks than the male customers. But male customers give more importance to certain service quality factors than the female customers. Hence, the study analyses the gender among the customers in the three groups of banks. The results are shown in Table 3.2.

Table 3.2: Distribution of the Customers Based on Gender

Sl. No.	Gender	Number of Customers in			Total
		PSBs	PrsBS	NPrSBs	
1.	Male	309	133	45	487
2.	Female	78	46	12	136
	Total	**387**	**179**	**57**	**623**

It is clear from the above table, that a maximum of 78.17 per cent of the customers are male customers. The number of male customers in PSBs constitutes 79.84 per cent to the total of 387 customers. Among the customers of PrSBs, the male customers constitute 74.30 per cent to its total whereas among the NPrSBs, the male customers constitute 78.95 per cent to the total of 57 customers. The present analysis reveals the dominance of male customers in all three groups of banks.

Nativity of the Customers

The nativity of the customers reveals whether the customers belong to urban or rural area. Since the expectation and perception on service quality factors among the urban customers is totally different from the rural customers, the present study has made an attempt on analyzing this aspect. Usually, the urban customers have more knowledge and exposure on banking and banking facilities than the rural customers. The distribution of customers on the basis of their nativity is illustrated in Table 3.3.

Table 3.3: Distribution of the Customers Based on Nativity

Sl. No.	Nativity	Number of Customers in			Total
		PSBs	PrsBS	NPrSBs	
1.	Urban	322	147	57	526
2.	Rural	65	32	–	97
	Total	**387**	**179**	**57**	**623**

The above table shows that the urban customers constitute 84.43 per cent to the total. Among the PSBs, the urban customers constitute 83.20 per cent of the total 387 customers. The urban customers belonging to PrSBs constitutes 82.12 per cent of the total 179 customers. Among the NprSBs, the urban customers constitute 100 per cent. It shows that all the customers of NPrSBs are urban customers.

The analysis reveals that the number of urban customers is high in all three groups of banks and there is no rural customer in NPrSBs.

Level of Education of the Customers

The level of education provides more knowledge and exposure on the competitive services offered by the commercial banks in the globalized scenario. Hence, the level of education of the customers is included as one of the profile variables. The highly educated customers may be more aware of competitive services and expect more from their banks compared to uneducated customers. The level of education of the customers is confined to less than 10th standard, 10th standard, higher secondary level, under-graduation, post graduation and professional education.

Table 3.4: Level of Education of the Customers

Sl. No.	Level of Education	Number of Customers in			Total
		PSBs	PrsBS	NPrSBs	
1.	Less than 10th standard	29	21	–	50
2.	10th standard	66	12	8	86
3.	Higher Secondary level	65	19	14	98
4.	Under graduation	112	84	13	209
5.	Post graduation	73	29	14	116
6.	Professional education	42	14	8	64
	Total	**387**	**179**	**57**	**623**

Table 3.4 explains the distribution of customers on the basis of their level of education. The dominant level of education among the customers is under-graduation and post graduation which constitute 33.55 and 18.62 per cent to their respective total. The number of customers with education less than 10th standard constitutes 8.03 per cent to the total. In the case of PSBs, the prominent levels of education among

the customers are under graduation and post graduation which constitute 28.94 and 18.86 per cent to their respective total. In the PrSBs, these two levels are also the same but constitute 46.93 and 16.20 per cent to their respective total. In the NPrSBs, these two levels are post graduation and higher secondary which constitute 24.56 and 24.56 per cent to their respective total.

Monthly Income of the Customers

It represents the income earned by the customers every month. Since, the income of the customers may have its own influence on their level of expectation and perception on the service quality factors, it is included as one of the profile variables. The higher income customers expect more and also personalized services from the commercial banks compared to others. The income among the customers is confined to less than Rs. 10,000, 10,000 to 15,000, 15,001 to 20,000, 20,001 to 25,000, 25,001 to 30,000 and above Rs. 30,000. The distribution of customers on the basis of their monthly income is given in Table 3.5.

Table 3.5: Distribution of the Customers Based on Monthly Income

Sl. No.	Monthly Income (in Rs.)	Number of Customers in			Total
		PSBs	PrsBS	NPrSBs	
1.	Less than 10,000	62	6	–	68
2.	10,000 to 15,000	86	14	3	103
3.	15,001 to 20,000	45	27	4	76
4.	20,001 to 25,000	53	52	3	108
5.	25,001 to 30,000	51	38	15	104
6.	Above 30,000	90	42	32	164
	Total	**387**	**179**	**57**	**623**

The important monthly income categories among the customers is above Rs. 30,000 and Rs. 20,001 to 25,000 which constitute 26.32 and 17.34 per cent to their respective total. The number of customers with the monthly income of less than Rs. 10,000 constitutes 10.91 per cent of the total. The most important monthly income category among the customers of PSBs is above Rs. 30,000 which constitutes 23.26 per cent of its total whereas in PrSBs, it is Rs. 20,000 to 25,000 constituting 29.05 per cent of its total. In the case of NPrSBs, the most important monthly income group is above Rs. 30,000 which constitutes 56.14 per cent of its total. The analysis reveals that the number of higher income customer is identified to be more in NPrSBs and PrsBs compared to PSBs.

Occupation of the Customers

The occupation of the customers reveals the nature of work done by the customers. Since, their occupation influences their expectation and perception on the service quality offered by the commercial banks, it is included as one of the profile variables. The occupation of the customers is confined to agriculture, agriculture allied occupations, private employment, government employment, professional jobs and business. The occupation of the customers is illustrated in Table 3.6.

Table 3.6: Customers Based on Occupation

Sl. No.	Occupation	Number of Customers in			Total
		PSBs	PrsBS	NPrSBs	
1.	Agriculture	42	23	3	68
2.	Agriculture Allied	76	14	4	94
3.	Private Employment	65	31	9	105
4.	Government Employment	59	29	7	95
5.	Professional jobs	43	32	16	91
6.	Business	102	50	18	170
	Total	**387**	**179**	**57**	**623**

The important occupations among the customer are business and private employment which constitute 27.29 and 16.85 per cent to their respective total. The number of customers occupied in agriculture constitutes 10.91 per cent of the total. The important occupations among the customers in PSBs are business and agriculture allied occupations which constitute 26.36 and 19.64 per cent to their respective total. In the PrSBs, the two important occupations are business and professional jobs which constitute 27.93 and 17.88 per cent to their respective total. In the NPrSBs, the prominent two occupations are also business and professional jobs which constitute 31.58 and 28.07 per cent to their respective total. The analysis reveals that there are more number of customers from agriculture and agriculture allied occupations in PSBs whereas in PrSBs and NPrSBs, there are more customers from business and professional jobs.

Years of Experience of the Customers

It represents the years of experience of customers in banking. Customers with more years of experience may have better idea on the service quality of commercial banks and hence it is included as one of the profile variables. The years of experience of the customers is confined to less than 2 years, 2 to 5 years, 6 to 9, 10 to 13, 14 to 17 and above 17 years. The distribution of customers on the basis of their years of experience is shown in Table 3.7. (*See Table on page 58*)

The important periods of experience among the customers are 10 to 13 years and above 17 years which constitute 23.75 and 21.67 per cent to their respective total. The number of customers with the experience of less than 2 years constitutes only 5.78 per cent of the total. The important periods of experience among the customers in PSBs are above 17 years and 10 to 13 years which constitute 26.36 and 22.99 per cent to their respective total. In PrSBs, the foremost periods of experience are 10 to 13 years and 6 to 9 years which constitute 24.56 and 21.05 per cent to their respective total. The analysis reveals that customers in PSBs are highly experienced whereas the customers in NPrSBs are less experienced.

Table 3.7: Distribution of Customers Based on Years of Experience in Banking

Sl. No.	Years of Experience	Number of Customers in			Total
		PSBs	PrsBS	NPrSBs	
1.	Less than 2 years	11	17	8	36
2.	2-5	48	23	11	82
3.	6-9	65	36	12	113
4.	10-13	89	45	14	148
5.	14-17	72	29	8	109
6.	Above 17	102	29	4	135
	Total	**387**	**179**	**57**	**623**

Classification of Customers

The customers are classified on the basis of their basic attitude towards the selection of the commercial bank. Even though, the variables included to select the commercial banks are too many, the present study is confined to nine variables. The customers are asked to rate the nine variables at five point scale. The assigned marks on these scales are 5 to 1 respectively. The score of nine variables have been included for the factor analysis to narrate the variables into factors. The test of validity of data for factor analysis has been conducted initially. The results are given in Table 3.8. (*See Table on page 59*)

The test of validity of data for factor analysis reveals the validity of data since the KMO measure is greater than zero per cent level and the level of significance of chi-square is at zero per cent level. The application of Exploratory Factor Analysis (EFA) results in two factors namely 'performance' and 'convenience'. The performance factor consists of six variables and their respective factor loadings are higher in this factor compared to another factor. The cronbach alpha reveals that the included six variables in this factor explain this factor to the extent of 79.68 per cent. The eigen value and the per cent of variation explained by this factor are 4.1128 and 51.63 per cent respectively. The most important variables in the 'performance' factor are service right at the first time, and competent employees for better performance since their respective factor loadings are 0.9123 and 0.8604 respectively.

Table 3.8: Variables Related to the Type of Customers

Sl. No.	Variables	Performance	Convenience
1.	Service right at the first time	0.9123	
2.	Competent employees for better performance	0.8604	
3.	Prompt service	0.7461	
4.	Courteous, friendly service	0.6862	
5.	Understanding customers' needs	0.6117	
6.	Competitive pricing	0.6008	
7.	Convenient location		0.9047
8.	Convenient hours of banking		0.8142
9.	Visually appealing facilities		0.7279
	Eigen value	4.1148	2.5644
	Per cent of variance explained	51.6324	27.6892
	Cronbach alpha	0.7968	0.6803
KMO Measure of sampling adequacy: 0.8142		Bartletts test of sphericity: chi-Square Value:103.39*	

* Significant at zero per cent level.

The second factor identified by the factor analysis is 'convenience' factor since its respective eigen value and the per cent of variation explained by this factor are 2.5644 and 27.6892 per cent respectively. The important variables in this factor are 'convenient location' and 'convenient hours' since their respective factor loadings are 0.9047 and 0.8142.

Reliability and Validity of the Variables in Each Factor

The reliability and validity of the two factors are tested with the help of Confirmatory Factor Analysis (CFA). The convergent validity and composite reliability have been examined with the help of the standardized factor loading and its significance and composite validity. The results are given in Table 3.9.

Table 3.9: Properties of Confirmatory Factor Analysis

Sl. No.	Factors and Variables	Standardised Factor Loading	t-Statistics	Composite Reliability Extracted in per cent	Average Variance
1	2	3	4	5	6
I.	**Performance**				
1.	Provide prompt service	0.7664	9.8664	0.8142	81.42
2.	Understand customer needs	0.8146	11.8969		
3.	Perform service right at first time	0.8029	10.2481		
4.	Offer competitive pricing	0.8445	12.1883		
5.	Have competent employees for better performance	0.9102	13.3446		

(Contd...)

1	2	3	4	5	6
6.	Provide courteous, friendly service	0.7601	9.0142		
II.	**Convenience**				
	Convenient operating hours	0.7334	8.5616	0.7969	73.62
	Convenient location	0.8642	13.0114		
	Provide visually appealing facilities	0.6996	8.0141		

* All 't' statistics are significant at five per cent level.

The two factor CFA analysis confirm the convergent validity and composite validity. Since, all standardized factor loadings of the variables are greater than 0.70 and their respective 't' statistics are significant at five per cent level, the convergent validity is confirmed. The composite validity shows the content validity of each factor since their reliability coefficients are greater than 0.70. The average variance explained by each factor is greater than the standard minimum of 50 per cent i.e 81.42 and 73.62 per cent. It reveals the content validity of the factor. The correlation between the performance and convenience factor is not statistically significant. It shows the discriminate validity. Hence, these two factors namely 'performance' and 'convenience' are taken as two different factors which determine the type of customers namely performance-seekers and convenience-seekers.

Score on Performance and Convenience

The score on performance and convenience is drawn from the mean score of the variables in each factor. The mean of score on performance and convenience among the customers in PSBs, PrSBs and NPrSBs have been computed and exhibited in Table 3.10.

Table 3.10: Score onPerformance and Convenience Among the Customers

Sl. No.	Type of Banks	Score on Performance		Mean	Standard deviation	Score on convenience		Mean	Standard deviation
		Minimum	Maximum						
1.	PSBs	2.8185	4.1786	3.6183	0.7879	1.8684	3.8781	3.0685	1.1446
2.	PrSBs	3.0445	4.3344	3.9244	1.3344	2.1145	3.6029	2.7339	0.8493
3.	NPrSBs	3.1146	4.1887	3.8061	1.0213	1.9314	3.9173	2.8186	0.5606

Table 3.10 shows that among the customers in PSBs, the mean score on performance factor is 3.6183 whereas the mean score on convenience factor is 3.0685. The standard deviations of the above two means are 0.7879 and 1.1446 respectively. Among the customers in PrSBs, the mean score on performance and convenience are 3.9244 and 2.7339 respectively with the standard deviation of 1.3344 and 0.8493 respectively. Among the customers in NPrSBs, mean scores are 3.8061 and 2.8186 respectively with the standard deviation of 1.0213 and 0.5606.

Type of Customers

The type of customers represents the customers who give more importance to 'performance' of the bank and 'convenience' of the bank. In the present study, the customers are classified on the basis of their mean score on performance and convenience. If their mean score on convenience is greater than the mean score on performance, they are treated as 'convenience-seekers. If the mean score on 'performance' is greater than the mean score on convenience, they are grouped as 'performance-seekers. The distribution of customers on the basis of their mean score is given in Table 3.11.

Table 3.11: Types of Customers

Sl. No.	Types of Customers	Number of customers in			Total
		PSBs	PrsBS	NPrSBs	
1.	Performance seekers	296	136	42	474
2.	Convenience seekers	91	43	15	149
	Total	**387**	**179**	**57**	**623**

The above table reveals that 76.08 per cent of the customers are performance seekers whereas only 23.92 per cent of the customers are convenience seekers. In Public Sector Banks, the performance seekers constitutes 76.48 per cent whereas only 23.52 per cent of the customers are convenience seekers. In the case of Private Sector Banks, the performance seekers constitute 75.98 per cent of the total of 179 customers. In the case of NPrSBs, performance seekers constitute 73.68 per cent of the total. The analysis reveals that majority of the customers are performance seekers.

Service Quality in Commercial Banks

The competitive climate in the Indian financial market has changed dramatically over the last few years. Business houses have entered into financial service activities. Public Sector Banks have started mutual fund trusts and other financial service subsidiaries. These subsidiaries have introduced new products in the market, which have competitive advantage over products of the banks. Even private sector foreign banks have introduced innovative activities. The expectations of the customers have also changed nowadays. Many consumers expect a variety of services from the banks. Many household consumers, now, prefer to take consumer durable loans or buy on instant credit rather than save for a few years to buy the consumer durable. As a result of this growing level of competition, service quality is emerging as an important element in banking activities. There is a need for the Indian Banks to keep pace with their competitors by using service quality techniques for business growth.

Service quality variables in commercial banks were identified by many researchers at so many dimensions.

The number of service quality variables, included in the present study, are 35. The customers have been asked to rate these 35 variables at five point scale on two dimensions namely expectation and perception. The scores of the variables on the perception dimensions alone have been included for the Exploratory Factor Analysis, to narrate the variables into factors because of the supremacy of performance measurement only. Initially, the test of validity of data for factor analysis has been conducted with the help of KMO measure of sampling adequacy and Bartletts test of Sphericity. Both these tests satisfy the validity of data for factor analysis. The variables which are having less than 0.5 as their factor loading in anyone of the extracted factors and the variables which are having greater than 0.5 as their factor loading in more than one factor are deleted from the factor analysis. Similarly, the criterion for accepting the factor is fixed as a minimum of 1.00 as its eigen value.

Out of the 35 variables included in the present study, 10 variables have been excluded from the exploratory factor analysis because of the above said two reasons. The variables having lesser factor loading (0.4) are reasonable fees and commission, good explanation of service fees, no delays due to bureaucratic factors, sufficient number of open tellers, decoration facilities and precision of account statement. The variables namely balance amount from which service charges begin, keeping the customers informed, waiting is not too long and queues that move rapidly are having higher factor loadings in more than one factor. The remaining 25 variables are narrated into five factors. The factor loading of the variables in the concerned factors is presented in Table 3.12. (*See Table on next page*)

The narrated five service quality factors explain the service quality variables to the extent of 74.62 per cent. The narrated five service quality factors consist of five service quality variables each. The most important service quality factor is 'reliability' since its eigen value and the per cent of variance explained are 4.8568 and 21.08 per cent respectively. The important service quality variables in reliability are 'service right at first time' and 'sincere in solving problems' since their respective factor loadings are 0.8684 and 0.8117 respectively.

Table 3.12: Factor Loading of Service Quality Variables for Underling Service Factors

Variables	Reliability	Responsiveness	Assurance	Tangibles	Empathy
Service Right at first time	0.8684				
Sincere in solving problem	0.8117				
Absence of error in service delivery	0.7336				
Sincere as per the promise	0.6819				
Precision filing system	0.6093				
Always willing to help customers		0.9163			
Communicate what to be served		0.8045			
Respond to customer's request		0.7139			
Prompt service		0.6342			
Never being too busy to respond customer's request		0.5446			
Feeling of security			0.9818		
Knowledgeable employees			0.7707		
Friendliness among employees			0.7316		

(Contd…)

Variables	Reliability	Responsiveness	Assurance	Tangibles	Empathy
Recognition of client			0.6494		
Consistently courteous with customers			0.5998		
Visually appealing equipment				0.8486	
Efficacious work environment				0.8019	
Precision of account statement				0.7234	
Cleanliness of facilities				0.6569	
Complementary equipments				0.6163	
Individual attention					0.9334
Informative					0.8664
Convenient operating hours and locations					0.7227
Customer's best interest at heart					0.7017
Understand specific needs					0.6149
Eigen value	4.8568	3.0441	2.4506	1.8969	1.0345
Per cent of variance explained	21.08	17.56	14.11	12.01	9.86
Cronbach alpha	0.7144	0.7213	0.7586	0.7617	0.8213
KMO: Measure of Sampling Adequacy: 0.7814	Bartletts test of sphericity: chi-Square: 98.92*				

Note: Factor loading less than 0.5 are not shown.

* Significant at zero per cent level.

The second factor identified by the factor analysis is 'responsiveness'. It consists of five variables with the reliability coefficient of 0.7213. It infers that the included five variables explain this factor to the extent of 72.13 per cent. The eigen value and the per cent of variance explained by this factor are 3.0441 and 17.56 per cent respectively. The important variables in this factor are 'always willing to help the customer' and 'communicate what to be served' since their factor loadings are 0.9163 and 0.8045 respectively.

The third factor narrated by the factor analysis is 'Assurance' factor since its eigen value and the per cent of variation explained by the factor are 2.4506 and 14.11 per cent respectively. The included service quality variables in this factor are five. The reliability coefficient of 0.7586 infers that the included five variables explain this factor to the extent of 75.86 per cent. The important variables in this factor are 'feeling of security' and 'knowledgeable employees' since their respective factor loadings are 0.9818 and 0.7707.

The fourth factor consists of five variables related to 'Tangibles' with the reliability coefficient of 0.7617. The eigen value and the per cent of variance explained by this factor are 1.8969 and 12.01 per cent respectively. The important variables in the 'Tangible' factor are 'visually appealing equipment' and 'efficacious of working environment' since their respective factor loadings are 0.8486 and 0.8019 respectively.

The last factor identified by the factor analysis is 'Empathy' since its eigen value and the per cent of variation explained by this factor are 1.0345 and 9.86 per cent respectively. The five variables included in this factor explain this factor to the extent of 82.13 per cent since its reliability coefficient is 0.8213. The important variables in this factor are 'individual attention' and 'informative' since their respective factor loadings are 0.9334 and 0.8664.

Validity and Reliability of Variables in the Five Service Quality Factors

The reliability of the variables included in each factor is tested with the help of the convergent validity and composite reliability. In order to analyse the validity of these two, Confirmatory Factory Analysis (CFA) has been administered. The score of the 25 variables under five factor models have been included for the present study. The standardized factor loading, its 't' statistics, composite reliability and average variance extracted are presented in Table 3.13.

Table 3.13: Properties of the Confirmatory Factor Analysis for SERVPERF

Sl. No.	Factors and Variables	Standardised Factor Loading	t-Statistics	Composite Reliability	Average Variance Extracted
1.	**Reliability**				
	Sincere as per the promise	0.7614	8.2141	0.982	0.8459
	Right at first time	0.8741	10.5817		
	Sincere in solving problem	0.8402	10.2402		
	Precision in filing system	0.8561	10.3331		
	Absence of error in service delivery	0.8809	11.0469		
2.	**Responsiveness**				
	Prompt service	0.9142	12.1703	0.960	0.8147
	Respond to customers' request	0.8319	9.4562		
	Always willing to help customers	0.8266	9.0444		
	Communicate what is to be served	0.7308	8.1149		

(Contd...)

Sl. No.	Factors and Variables	Standardised Factor Loading	t-Statistics	Composite Reliability	Average Variance Extracted
	Never being too busy to respond to customers request	0.6617	7.5161		
3.	**Assurance**				
	Knowledgeable employees	0.8817	11.0868	0.964	0.8216
	Consistently courteous with customers	0.6903	8.0433		
	Recognition of client	0.9144	12.6566		
	Feeling of security	0.6814	7.9343		
	Friendliness among employees	0.7809	8.4143		
4.	**Tangibles**				
	Precision account statement	0.8214	8.9141	0.981	0.8339
	Efficacious work environment	0.8006	8.5063		
	Visually appealing equipment	0.9149	13.1718		
	Cleanliness of facilities	0.8767	10.7334		
	Complementary equipments	0.7338	8.3037		
5.	**Empathy**				
	Understand specific needs	0.9106	11.3364	0.967	0.8231
	Individual attention	0.8024	8.6161		
	Informative	0.7334	8.2162		

(Contd...)

Sl. No.	Factors and Variables	Standardised Factor Loading	t-Statistics	Composite Reliability	Average Variance Extracted
	Convenient operating hours and location	0.8616	10.2451		
	Customer's best interest at heart	0.6887	8.0042		
	Overall composite reliability:0.8449				

* All 't' statistics are significant at five per cent level.

The standardised factor loading of the variables associated in each factor is greater than 0.66 and the 't' statistics of the standardized factor loading of the variables in each factor is significant at five per cent level. It shows the covergent validity of the variables included in each factor. The composite reliability of each factor also indicates the reliability of the variables included in each factor. The minimum acceptable composite reliability is 0.50. In this case, the composite validity of the factors is greater than 0.5. Hence, the content validity is assured. The average variance extracted by each factor is also varying from 0.8147 to 0.8459. All these indicate the validity and reliability of the service quality factors for further analysis.

Discriminate Validity of the Service Quality Factors (SQFs)

The discriminate validity of the SQFs have been computed to analyse the level of mutual exclusiveness among the service quality factors. In order to test the discriminate validity, the scores of the SQFs have been computed from the mean score of the SQ variables included in each factor. The scores of service quality factors are included for the correlation analysis to exhibit the inter correlation between the service quality factors. The discriminate validity is assured when the inter correlation coefficients are not statistically significant. The computed inter correlation coefficients among the service quality factors are summarized in Table 3.14.

Table 3.14: Correlation Among Latent Constructs

SQFs	Reliability	Responsiveness	Assurance	Tangibles	Empathy
Reliability		0.2414	0.1809	0.1234	0.2109
Responsiveness			0.2617	0.1881	0.0864
Assurance				0.2172	0.1434
Tangibles					0.2636
Empathy					

The inter-correlation coefficient among the SQFs is ranging from 0.0864 to 0.2636. The higher correlation is identified between tangibles and empathy since its correlation coefficient is 0.2636. It is followed by 'responsiveness' and 'assurance' with its correlation coefficient being 0.2617. The lowest correlation is identified between responsiveness and empathy since the correlation coefficient is 0.0864. But all inter correlation coefficients are not statistically significant, it justifies the discriminate validity among the five service quality factors.

Customers' Expectation on SQFs

The customers' expectation on the SQFs in commercial banks has been estimated by the mean score of the variables included in each factor. The mean of the five service quality factors, among the customers in PSBs, PrSBs and NPrSBs have been estimated to exhibit their level of expectation. The one way analysis of variance has been executed to find out the significant difference among the three groups of customers regarding their level of expectations. The results are given in Table 3.15.

Table 3.15: Expectation on SQFS Among Customers

Sl. No.	SQFs	Mean Score Among Customers in			F-Statistics
		PSBs	PrsBS	NPrSBs	
1.	Reliability	3.4547	3.8185	4.0617	1.3446
2.	Responsiveness	3.6068	3.9293	3.8568	0.9182
3.	Assurance	3.7516	3.8068	4.1423	0.6863
4.	Tangibles	3.2447	3.4017	3.3887	0.3916
5.	Empathy	3.8108	3.9239	4.1143	0.4024

The highly expected service quality among the customers in PSBs is "Empathy and Assurance" since their respective mean scores are 3.8108 and 3.7516 respectively. Among the customers in PrSBs these service quality factors are 'Responsiveness and Empathy' since their respective mean scores are 3.9239 and 3.9293. The highly expected service quality factors among the customers in NPrSBs is 'Assurance' and 'Empathy' since their respective mean scores are 4.1423 and 4.1143. In total, the customers in NPrSBs are expecting more than the customers in the other two groups of banks. Since the 'F' statistics is not statistically significant, the analysis reveals that there is significant difference among the three groups of customers regarding their level of expectation.

SERVPERF Scale on SQFs Among the Customers

The measurement of perception on the service quality factors is treated as SERVPERF scale on SQFs. In the present study, the level of perception on the five SQFs among the customers in PSBs, PrSBs and NPrSBs has been computed separately to identify the level of perception on SQFs among the three groups of customers. The one way analysis of variance is administered to find out the significant difference among the customers in the three groups of banks. The results are presented in Table 3.16.

Table 3.16: Perception of SQFS (SERVPERF Scale) Among Customers

Sl. No.	SQFs	Mean score among customers in			F-Statistics
		PSBs	PrsBS	NPrSBs	
1.	Reliability	2.5146	3.6237	3.7145	3.8442*
2.	Responsiveness	2.7208	3.6669	3.4039	3.2968*
3.	Assurance	2.5064	3.3234	3.6256	3.3916*
4.	Tangibles	2.6567	3.2186	3.1617	0.9168
5.	Empathy	2.7183	3.1146	3.8089	2.9901*

* Significant at five per cent level.

In general, the level of perception is lesser than the level of expectation on all SQFs since the level of perception on SQFs is varying from 2.5064 to 3.8089. The highly perceived SQFs by the customers in PSBs are 'responsiveness' and 'empathy' since their mean scores are 2.7208 and 2.7183 respectively. Among the customers in PrSBs, these SQFs are 'Responsiveness and Reliability' since their respective mean scores are 3.6669 and 3.6237. Among the customers in NPrSBs, these SQFs are Empathy and reliability since their respective mean scores are 3.8083 and 3.7145 respectively. Regarding the perception on service quality factors the customers in NPrSBs rate the SQFs at higher rate than their counterparts. The significant differences among the three groups of customers have been identified in perception on reliability, responsiveness, assurance and empathy since their respective 'F' statistics are significant at five per cent level.

SERVQUAL Score on SQFs Among the Customers

The SERVQUAL score is the difference between the customer's perception and expectation on SQFs. The positive SERVQUAL score indicates that the customers are satisfied over and above their expectations on SQFs. The negative SERVQUAL score reveals that the customers are not satisfied upto their level of expectation. The mean of SERVQUAL scores on five SQFs among the customers in PSBs, PrSBs and NPrSBs have been computed to exhibit the level of difference between their perception and expectation. In order to find out the significant difference among the three groups of customers regarding their SERVQUAL score on SQFs, the one way analysis of variance has been executed. The results are given in Table 3.17.

Table 3.17: SERVQUAL Score Among the Customers

Sl. No.	SQFs	Mean Score among Customers in			F-Statistics
		PSBs	PrsBS	NPrSBs	
1.	Reliability	-0.9401	-0.1948	-0.3472	3.3862*
2.	Responsiveness	-0.8860	-0.2624	-0.4529	3.7129*
3.	Assurance	-1.2452	-0.4834	-0.5167	3.0144*
4.	Tangibles	-0.5880	-0.1837	-0.2270	1.2345
5.	Empathy	-1.0925	-0.5093	-0.3054	3.1496*

* Significant at five per cent level.

The SERVQUAL score on five SQFs among all three groups of customers are in negative. It represents that the customers are not satisfied upto their level of expectation on all five SQFs. Among the customers in PSBs, the highest difference between the perception and expectation is identified in the case of 'assurance' and 'empathy' since their respective SERVQUAL scores are -1.2452 and -1.0925. Among the customers in PrSBs, the highest difference is identified in 'empathy' and 'assurance' since their respective SERVQUAL scores are -0.5093 and -0.4834. In the NPrSBs, the highest SERVQUAL scores have been noticed in the case of 'assurance' and 'responsiveness' since their respective mean scores are -0.5167 and -0.4529. Regarding the SERVQUAL scores, the significant difference among the three groups of customers has been noticed in the case of reliability, responsiveness, assurance and empathy since their respective 'F' statistics are significant at five per cent level.

Customer Satisfaction

The customer satisfaction is the collective opinion on various aspects in commercial banks. The primary motto of any commercial banks in the globalized era is customer satisfaction. Even though the customer satisfaction is derived from the customers' attitude towards various variables related to banks, the present study has been confined to only 12 variables. These variables are given in Table 3.18.

Table 3.18: Variables in Customer's Satisfaction

Sl. No.	Variables
1.	Decision to use the bank
2.	Experience with the bank
3.	My choice towards the bank
4.	Employee behaviour
5.	Accessibility of the bank
6.	Trust worthiness of the bank
7.	Relationship-marketing adopted by the bank
8.	Customers' orientation of the bank
9.	Handling of complaints
10.	Reporting system of the bank
11.	Quality of service
12.	Cost of the services offered

The identified variables are related to the service offered by the banks, service providers (employees) and service cost. The customers are asked ro rank the twelve variables at five point scale. The assigned scores on these scales are from 5 to 1 respectively. The scores have been included for exploratory factor analysis to narrate the variables into factors. Initially, the validity and reliability have been confirmed with the help of KMO measure of sampling adequacy and the Bartletts test of Sphericity.

Application of Exploratory Factor Analysis

Initially, the test of validity of data for factor analysis have been conducted with the help of KMO measure and Bartletts test of Sphericity. Both the KMO measure of sampling adequacy and chi-square value satisfy the validity of data for factor analysis. The score of the twelve variables have been included for the Exploratory Factor Analysis (EFA). The result of EFA is illustrated in Table 3.19.

Table 3.19: Factor Loading of the Variables in Customers Satisfaction

Sl. No.	Variables	Employee	Bank
1.	Customers orientation	0.9247	
2.	Relationship marketing	0.8108	
3.	Employee behaviour	0.7633	
4.	Quality of service	0.7217	
5.	Handling complaints	0.6804	
6.	Accessibility	0.6116	
7.	Experience with the bank		0.8969
8.	Choice of the bank		0.8305
9.	Trust worthiness of the bank		0.8144
10.	Reporting system of the bank		0.7603
11.	Cost of services offered		0.7117
12.	Decision to use the bank		0.6554
	Eigen value	5.0443	4.4568
	Per cent of variance explained	39.3817	34.0671
	Cronbach alpha	0.8144	0.8646
KMO Measure of Sampling Adequacy: 0.7449		Bartletts test of sphericity: chi-square value: 84.08*	

* Significant at zero per cent level.

The twelve variables are narrated into two factors namely employee and bank. These two factors explain the twelve variables to the extent of 73.45 per cent. The most important factor is 'employee' since its eigen value and the per cent of variation explained by this factor are 5.0443 and 39.38 per cent respectively. The employee factor consists of six variables with the reliability coefficient of 0.8144. It reveals that the included six variables explain this factor to the extent of 81.44 per cent. The next factor identified by the factor analysis is 'bank' since its eigen value and the per cent of variation explained by this factor are 4.4568 and 34.0671 respectively. The included six variables explain this factor to the extent of 86.46 per cent since their respective cronbach alpha is 0.8646. These two factors have been included for further analysis.

Reliability and Validity of the Variables in the Factors

The Confirmatory Factor Analysis (CFA) has been administered to examine the reliability and validity of the variables in each factor. The convergent validity, composite reliability and average variance extracted are computed with the help of CFA. The results are given in Table 3.20. (*See on next page*)

Since all standardized factor loadings are higher than 0.70 and the 't' statistics of the variables are significant at five per cent level of significance, the convergent validity of the variables in each factor is confirmed. The composite reliability of the two factors confirms its reliability since the reliability coefficients are higher than the standard minimum of 0.70. The overall composite reliability of the variables is also higher than the minimum threshold of 0.7. The average variance extracted by these two factors are 0.8445 and 0.8961 respectively. In order to test the discriminate validity of the two factors, the correlation between the factors of 'employee' and 'bank' has been computed. The significant high correlation is identified between these two factors. Hence, the study infers that there is no discrimination between the 'employee' and 'bank' factors. Hence, the customer satisfaction is computed by the score of all 12 variables in customer satisfaction.

Table 3.20: Properties of the Confirmatory Factor Analysis for Customer Satisfaction

Sl. No.	Factors and Variables	Standardised Factor Loading	t-Statistics	Composite Reliability	Average Variance Extracted
I	**Employee**	0.8184	10.1124	0.9147	0.8445
	Relationship marketing	0.7643	9.2746		
	Employee behaviour	0.8969	12.6443		
	Quality of service	0.8402	10.3441		
	Handling complaints	0.7606	9.1034		
	Accessibility	0.7314	8.9317		
	Customer orientation	0.7226	8.2042		
II	**Bank**				
	Choice of thebank	0.9146	13.0869	0.9646	0.8961
	Decision to use the bank	0.8673	11.4557		
	Reporting system of the bank	0.7229	8.6817		
	Trust worthiness of the bank	0.8501	10.6937		
	Cost of services offered	0.8952	12.0431		
	Experience with the bank	0.7144	8.1141		
Overall composite reliability:0.8449					

Customer Satisfaction Index (CSI) among the Customers

Since there is no discrimination between the 'employee' and 'bank' factors in customers satisfaction, the customer satisfaction is derived from the score of all 12 variables included in it. The score of customer satisfaction is summated with the help of an index called 'Customer Satisfaction Index' (CSI). It is computed by:

$$CSI = \frac{\sum_{i=1}^{n} SVCS_i}{\sum_{i=1}^{n} MSVCS_i} \times 100$$

where

SVCS – Score of variables in customer satisfaction

MSVCS – Maximum score of the variables in customer satisfaction

I=1…n – Variables in customer satisfaction

The distribution of customers on the basis of their CSI is shown in Table 3.21.

Table 3.21: Customer Satisfaction Index (CSI) Among the Customers

Sl. No.	CSI (in per cent)	Number of customers in			Total
		PSBs	PrsBS	NPrSBs	
1.	Less than 21	70	11	4	85
2.	21-40	139	26	12	177
3.	41-60	113	49	11	173
4.	61-80	38	57	13	108
5.	Above 80	27	36	17	80
	Total	**387**	**179**	**57**	**623**

The important CSI among the customers are 21 to 40 and 41 to 60 per cent since they constitute 28.41 and 27.77 per cent to their respective total. The number of customers with an index of above 80 per cent constitutes 12.84 per cent to the total. The most important CSI among the customers in PSBs is 21 to 40 per cent which constitutes 35.92 per cent of its total whereas among the customers in PrSBs, it is 61 to 80 per cent which constitutes 31.84 per cent of its total. Among the customers in NPrSBs, it is above 80 per cent which constitutes 29.82 per cent of its total. The analysis reveals that the customer satisfaction is higher among the customers of NPrSBs as compared to the customers of PrSBs and PSBs.

Impact of SERVPERF Scale on SQFs on CSI

The perception on SQFs may have its own influence on the customer satisfaction. In order to analyse the impact of each SQF on customer satisfaction among the customers, the multiple regression analysis has been administered. The fitted regression model is

$$Y = a+b_1X_1+b_2X_2+b_3X_3+b_4X_4+b_5X_5+e$$

where

X_1 – Score on Reliability among the customers

X_2 – Score on Responsiveness among the customers

X_3 – Score on Assurance among the customers

X_4 – Score on Tangibles among the customers

X_5 – Score on Empathy among the customers

$b_1, b_2 \ldots b_n$ – Regression coefficients of independent variables

a – Intercept and

e – Error term

Table 3.22: Impact of SERVPERF Scale on SQFS on CSI

Sl. No.	SQFs	Regression Co-efficients among Customers in		
		PSBs	PrSBs	NPrSBs
1.	Reliability	0.1814*	0.2492*	0.2096*
2.	Responsiveness	0.0933	0.1891*	0.1443*
3.	Assurance	0.1044	0.1044	0.1862*
4.	Tangibles	0.1133	0.1338*	0.2101*
5.	Empathy	0.1681*	0.2096*	0.2633*
	Constant	0.9194	1.3039	1.5238
	R2	0.6345	0.7569	0.7161
	F-Statistics	8.0828*	11.1083*	9.8689*

* Significant at five per cent level.

The SQFs significantly influencing on the CSI among the customers in PSBs are reliability and empathy. A unit increase in the perception on reliability and empathy results in an increase in CSI among the customers in PSBs by 0.1814 and 0.1681 units respectively. Among the customers in PrSBs, the significantly influencing SQFs are the perception on reliability, responsiveness, tangibles and empathy since their respective regression coefficients are significant at five per cent level. A unit increase in the perception on the above said SQFs results in an increase in CSI by 0.2492, 0.1891, 0.1338 and 0.2096 units respectively. Among the customers in NPrSBs, a unit increase in the perception on reliability, responsiveness, assurance, tangibles and empathy results in an increase in customer satisfaction index by 0.2096, 0.1443, 0.1862, 0.2101 and 0.2633 units respectively. The changes in the perception on SQFs explain the changes in CSI among the customers in PSBs and PrSBs is to the extent of 63.45 and 75.69 per cent respectively, but among the customers in NPrSBs, it is to the extent of 71.61 per cent. The analysis reveals the importance of SQFs in customer satisfaction. The significant 'F' statistics reveal the validity of fitted regression models.

Discriminate SQFs Among the Customers in the Three Groups of Commercial Banks

The customers belong to Public Sector, Private Sector and New Private Sector Banks. The customer's perception on the service quality factors in the three groups of banks may differ. It is highly imperative to identify the important discriminate SQFs among the customers in the three groups of banks for some policy implications. In order to identify these discriminate SQFs, the Multi-Discriminate Analysis has been administered. The multi discriminate model involves linear combinations in the following form:

$$Z=b_0+b_1X_1+b_2X_2+b_3X_3+b_4X_5+b_5X_5$$

where

Z	–	Discriminate Score
$X_1, X_2 \ldots X_5$	–	Service Quality Factors
$b_1, b_2 \ldots . b_5$	–	Discriminate coefficients or weights
b0	–	Intercept

Initially, the mean score on the perception on each dimension of service quality, has been computed among the customers in the three groups of banks. Their significant difference is examined with the help of one way analysis of variance. The discriminate power of each Service Quality Factor is analysed with the help of its Wilk's Lambda. The results are given in Table 3.23. (*See Table on next page*)

The above table shows that the customers in NPrSBs have more perception on the service quality offered by their banks since their mean scores on reliability, assurance and empathy are higher than the customers in the other two groups of banks. The customers in PrSBs have more perception on the factors of 'responsiveness' and 'tangibles' of their banks compared to their counterparts. The customers in PSBs show poor perception on the service quality of their banks. The significant mean difference among the three groups of customers has been noticed in the perception on

Table 3.23: Mean Difference and Discriminate Power of SQFS

Sl. No.	SQFs	Mean Score among customers in			F-Statistics	P-value	Wilk's Lambda
		PSBs	PrSBs	NPrSBs			
1.	Reliability	2.5146	3.6237	3.7145	3.8442	0.0039	0.1451
2.	Responsiveness	2.7208	3.6669	3.4039	3.2968	0.0322	0.3129
3.	Assurance	2.5064	3.3234	3.6256	3.3916	0.0211	0.2962
4.	Tangibles	2.6567	3.2186	3.1617	0.9198	0.2568	0.4561
5.	Empathy	2.1783	3.4146	3.8089	2.9901	0.0419	0.1233

reliability, responsiveness, assurance and empathy since their respective 'F' statistics are significant at five per cent level. The lower Wilk's Lambda indicates the higher discriminate power of the SQFs. In the present study, higher discriminate power is identified in the case of empathy and reliability since their respective Wilk's Lambda are 0.1233 and 0.1451. It is concluded that the three groups of banks are highly discriminated by the perception on the factors of 'empathy' and 'reliability' among the customers. Regarding these two SQFs, the NPrSBs are better than PrSBs which in turn are better than PSBs.

Canonical Discriminate Functions

In multi-discriminate analysis of three groups, G-1 discriminate function can be estimated if the number of discriminate variables is larger than the number of groups. In general, with 'G' groups and 'k' discriminate variables it is possible to estimate upto the smaller of G-1 or 'k' discriminate functions. The first function has the highest ratio between groups, to within group sum of squares. The second function uncorrelated with the first, has the second highest ratio, and so on. However, not all the functions may be statistically significant. In the present study, the number of groups is three namely PSBs, PrSBs and NPrSBs; and hence a maximum of two functions can be extracted. The result of these functions are given in Table 3.24. (*See Table on next page*)

The Eigen value associated with the first function is 4.8188 and this accounts for 92.04 per cent of the explained variance. Because of the higher eigen value, the first function is declared as superior. The second function has a small eigen value of 0.5177 and accounts for only 7.96 per cent of the explained variance. The '0' below after function indicates that no functions have been removed. The value of Wilk's Lambda is 0.1339. This transforms to a chi-square of 46.3949 which is significant at zero per cent level. Thus, the two functions, together, significantly discriminate the three groups of customers. However, the Wilk's Lambda of the

Table 3.24: Canonical Discriminate Function

Function	Eigen value	Per cent of variance	Cumulative per cent of variance	Canonical correlation	After function	Wilk's Lambda	Chi-Square value	P-Value
1.	4.8188	92.04	92.04	0.8139	0	0.1339	46.3949	0.0000
2.	0.5177	7.96	100.00	0.3914	1	0.8614	3.9193	0.3914

second function is 0.8614, which is not significant at five per cent level. Therefore, the second function is declared to be not contributing significantly to the group differences.

Discriminate Co-efficient of the various SQFs

The standardized discriminate function is estimated to find out the discriminate coefficient of the five SQFs. It is computed to identify the importance of discriminate SQFs among the customers in PSBs, PrSBs and NPrSBs. Since the multi-discriminate analysis results in two discriminate functions, the discriminate coefficients of SQFs in function-1 and function-2 are established. The results are presented in Table 3.25.

Table 3.25: Standardised Canonical Discriminate Function Coefficients

Sl. No.	SQFs	Function	
		Function-1	Function-2
1.	Reliability	0.3949	-0.1039
2.	Responsiveness	0.1437	0.4102
3.	Assurance	0.4971	0.5689
4.	Tangibles	-0.1039	0.1233
5.	Empathy	1.0345	0.2309
Per cent of cases correctly classified		79.03	28.03

Since the function-1 is already declared as the superior function because of its statistical significance, the function-1 alone is taken for the interpretation. According to the function-1, the important discriminate SQFs among the customers in PSBs, PrSBs and NPrSBs are empathy, assurance and reliability since their respective discriminate coefficients are 1.0345, 0.4971 and 0.3949. The analysis reveals that the customers in the three groups of banks are significantly and highly discriminated on the basis of the above said factors. Hence, the bank managers have to concentrate on these aspects to achieve like the other groups of banks.

Demographic Discriminators of Service Quality in the Banking Industry

Commercial banks that excel in quality service can have a distinct marketing edge, since improved cross-sell ratios, higher customer retention (Bennett and Higgins, 1988)[1], and expanded market share (Bowen and Hedges, 1993). Similarly, Easingwood and Storey (1993) reported that the total quality is the most important factor in the success of new financial services, while Bennett and Higgins (1988) believe that a competitive edge in banking originates almost exclusively from service quality.

Although service quality in banking has been considered as important over the years, the topic has recently been afforded even more attention. Such interest may be the result of reduced customer base and decreased market share affecting a portion of the banking industry (Bower and Hedges, 1993).[2] In fact, Bowen and Hedges believe that the attention to service quality may contribute substantially to ameliorating the decrease in market share that banks might be experiencing. Hence, achieving superior levels of service quality is a principal objective for retail banking operations.

Demographics continue to be one of the most popular and well accepted bases for segmenting markets and customers (Belch and Belch, 1993). Moreover, demographics are easier to measure than other segmentation variables. The service expectations among the customers with different demographic profiles is more important to place a right product/service to the right consumers at the right time. Previous research has shown that demographic variables are related to service quality expectations (Gagliano and Hathcote, 1994)[3]. Webster (1989)[4] found that age, gender and income were significantly related to service quality expectations for professional services. Hence, to discriminate among different demographic groups, the segmentation variables namely nativity, age, gender, education, income, type of customers, occupation and years of experience are used in the current study.

Nativity As a Discriminator of Service Quality

The 'nativity' indicates the urban and rural base of the customers. The nativity among the customers plays an important role in their level of expectations on service quality of the commercial banks because their level of expectation, exposure and knowledge on the banking environment among the customers is totally different among different groups. The present analysis has made an attempt to analyse how the nativity among the customers discriminate their service quality expectations for some policy implications.

Customers' Expectation on Service Quality

The customers' expectation on SQFs in commercial banks among the urban and rural customers has been estimated with the mean scores of the variables in each factor. The 't' statistics have been computed to analyse the significant difference among the two groups of customers regarding their level of expectation on SQFs. The results are given in Table 4.1.

Table 4.1: Customers' Expectation on Service Quality

Sl. No.	Service quality factors	Mean score among customers in		T-Statistics
		Urban	Rural	
1.	Reliability	3.9314	2.9481	2.9197*
2.	Responsiveness	3.9103	3.1864	2.0884*
3.	Assurance	4.0869	2.8877	3.2109*
4.	Tangibles	3.6913	2.1435	3.6446*
5.	Empathy	4.2088	2.5440	4.2617*

* Significant at five per cent level.

The number of urban and rural customers in the present study are 526 and 97 respectively. In general, the level of expectation on SQFs among the urban customers is greater than that among the rural customers. Among the urban customers, the highly expected SQFs are 'empathy' and 'assurance' since their respective mean scores are 4.2088 and 4.0869. Among the rural customers, the highly expected SQFs are 'responsiveness' and 'reliability' since its mean scores are 3.1864 and 2.9481 respectively. Regarding the level of expectation, the significant difference among the urban and rural customers has been identified in the expectation on all five SQFs since their respective 't' statistics are significant at five per cent.

Mean Difference and Discriminant Power of SQFs Among Urban and Rural Customers

The analysis has been made to identify the important discriminant SQFs among the urban and rural customers. The two group discriminant analysis has been executed to identify such SQFs. Initially, the mean difference among the urban and rural customer regarding their level of expectations, mean difference, statistical significance and discriminant power of the SQFs has been computed and shown in Table 4.2.

Table 4.2: Mean Difference and Discriminate Power of SQFS (Based on Expectations)

Sl. No.	SQFs	Mean of expectation among customer in		Mean Difference	't' Statistics	Wilks Lambda
		Urban	Rural			
1.	Reliability	3.9314	2.9481	0.9833	2.9197*	0.1969
2.	Responsiveness	3.9103	3.1864	0.7239	2.0884*	0.2168
3.	Assurance	4.0869	2.8877	1.1992	3.2109*	0.1708
4.	Tangibles	3.6913	2.1435	1.5478	3.6446*	0.2962
5.	Empathy	4.2088	2.5440	1.6648	4.2617*	0.1041

The significant mean difference among the urban and rural customer has been noticed in all five SQFs since their respective mean difference are significant at five per cent level. Higher mean difference is noticed in the case of empathy, tangibles and assurance since their respective mean differences are 1.6648, 1.5478 and 1.1992. Higher discriminant power of the SQFs is identified in the case of 'empathy' and 'assurance' since their respective Wilk's Lambda are 0.1041 and 0.1708 respectively. All the five SQFs are included to establish the two group discriminant function. The unstandardised procedure is followed to establish such function. The estimated function is

$$Z = 1.3034 + 0.3969\ X_1 + 0.2411\ X_2 + 0.3042\ X_3 + 0.1446\ X_4 + 0.2717\ X_5$$

The relative contribution of the service quality factors in total discriminant score is computed by the product of the discriminant co-efficients and their respective mean difference of the SQFs. The results are given in Table 4.3. (*See Table on next page*)

The highly influencing SQFs in discriminant function are reliability and assurance since their respective discriminant co-efficients are 0.3969 and 0.3042. The higher relative contribution of SQFs in TDS is noticed in the case of empathy and reliability since their respective contributions are 28.16 and 24.31 per cent. The analysis reveals that the urban customers are highly expecting reliability and empathy than the rural customers from their service providers. Hence the service providers understand this fact and design appropriate service strategy.

Table 4.3: Relative Contribution of Discriminant SQFS in Total Discriminant Score

Sl. No.	SQFs	Discriminant Co-efficient	Mean Difference	Product	Relative Contribution in TDS
1.	Reliability	0.3969	0.9833	0.3903	24.31
2.	Responsiveness	0.2411	0.7239	0.1745	10.87
3.	Assurance	0.3042	1.1992	0.3648	22.72
4.	Tangibles	0.1446	1.5478	0.2238	13.94
5.	Empathy	0.2717	1.6048	0.4523	28.16
	Total			**1.6057**	**100.00**

Per cent of cases correctly classified: 73.39.

Age As a Discriminator of Service Quality Expectation

Age is one of the important predictors of service quality expectation among the customers. The youngsters are more energetic and enthusiastic to learn the existing globalised banking environment. Naturally, they expect more service and service quality at the international level. The young customers never hesitate to switchover to other banks which provide better service. The aged customers are more experienced and loyal customers to the banks. They also expect more core products and services from the banks. But the level of expectation among the customers may be highly influenced by the age of the customer (Lassar, et al., 2000;

Gani and Mushtag, 2003). Hence, the present study has made an attempt to analyse the important discriminant SQFs among the different aged customers. The customers are classified into youngsters (less than 36 years), middle aged (36 to 55 years) and aged (above 56 years).

Customers' Expectation on SQFs among Different Age Groups of Customers

The expectation on SQFs among the different age groups may differ from one another. It is highly imperative to exhibit the level of expectation on SQFs among the three different age groups for some policy implications. The expectation score on the five SQFs has been derived from the mean score of the variables in each factor. The mean score of five SQFs among youngsters, middle aged and aged customers have been examined to exhibit their level of expectations on SQFs. The oneway analysis of variance has been administered to find out the significant difference among the three groups.

Table 4.4: Customers Expectation in Service Quality

Sl. No.	SQFs	Mean Scores among			F-Statistics
		Young	Middle Aged	Aged	
1.	Reliability	4.2086	3.8187	3.0719	4.2344*
2.	Responsiveness	4.1447	3.7402	3.4039	3.0969*
3.	Assurance	4.2723	3.6551	3.7827	3.1664*
4.	Tangibles	3.8559	3.3409	3.0443	3.1146*
5.	Empathy	3.8434	3.8686	4.2109	1.3417

* Significant at five per cent level.

The number of customers belonging to the young, middle aged and aged groups are 217, 259 and 147 customers. The highly expected SQFs among the youngsters are assurance and reliability since their respective mean scores are 4.2723 and 4.2086 respectively. Among the middle aged, the two highly expected SQFs are empathy and reliability since their respective mean scores are 3.8686 and 3.8187. The highly expected SQFs among the aged customers are empathy and assurance since their respective mean scores are 4.2109 and 3.7827. Regarding the level of expectation on SQFs, the significant difference among the three age groups is noticed in the case of reliability, responsiveness assurance and tangibles since their respective 'F' statistics are significant at five per cent level.

Mean Difference and Discriminant Power of SQFs

The service quality expectations among the three age groups of customers have been examined with the help of the mean score on level of expectation on five SQFs among the three groups of customers. The significant difference among them is analysed with the help of oneway analysis of variance. The discriminant power of the SQFs has been measured with the help of Wilks Lambda. The results are given in Table 4.5.

Table 4.5: Mean Difference and Discriminant Power of SQFS (Based on Expectations)

Sl. No.	SQFs	Mean of Expectation among Customer in			F-Statistics	P Value	Wilks Lambda
		Youngsters	Middle Aged	Aged			
1.	Reliability	4.2086	3.8187	3.0719	4.2344	0.0129	0.1234
2.	Responsiveness	4.1447	3.7302	3.4039	3.0969	0.0344	0.1687
3.	Assurance	4.2723	3.6551	3.7827	3.1664	0.0244	0.1441
4.	Tangibles	3.8559	3.3409	3.0443	3.1146	0.0299	0.2569
5.	Empathy	3.8434	3.8686	4.2109	1.3417	0.2816	0.4568

The significant difference among the three age groups of customers has been noticed in the case of reliability, responsiveness, assurance and tangibles since their respective 'F' statistics are significant at five per cent level. The higher expectation among the young customers is noticed in 'assurance' since its mean score is 4.2723 whereas among the middle aged, it is identified in 'empathy' since its mean score is 3.8686. Among the aged customers, it is identified in 'empathy' since its mean score is 4.2109. The higher discriminant power of the SQFs is noticed in reliability, assurance and responsiveness since their respective Wilks Lambda are 0.1234, 0.1441 and 0.1687.

Canonical Discriminant Functions

The present study consists of three age groups of customers. The multi-discriminant analysis has been administered to identify the discriminant functions. The standardized procedure has been followed to establish such functions. In total, a maximum of (G-1) functions can be generated. Hence, the present Multi Discriminant Analysis has generated two functions. The reliability and validity of these two functions are examined with the help of its eigen value and the per cent of variance. The results are presented in Table 4.6. (*See Table on next page*)

The eigen value associated with the first function is 4.9142 and this accounts for 85.61 per cent of the explained variance. Because of the high eigen value, the first function is declared to be superior than the second function. The second function has a smaller eigen value of 0.7133 and accounts for only 14.39 per cent of the explained variance. The '0' below after function indicates that no function has removed. The value of Wilk's Lambda is 0.1403. This transforms to a chi-square of 52.6108 which is significant at zero per cent level. Thus the functions together, significantly discriminate the three different age groups of customers. However, the Wilk's Lambda of the second function is 0.5681, which is not significant at five per cent level. Therefore, the second function is declared to be not contributing significantly on group differences.

Table 4.6: Cannonical Discriminant Function

Function	Eigen Value	Per cent of Variance	Cumulative Per cent of Variance	Canonical Correlation	After Function	Wilks Lambda	Chi-square Value	P Value
1.	4.9142	85.61	85.61	0.8102	0	0.1403	52.6108	0
2.	0.7133	14.39	100.00	0.2049	1	0.5681	1.9697	0.6844

Discriminant Co-efficient of the SQFs

The discriminant co-efficients of the SQFs have been computed with the help of multi discriminant analysis. The standardized procedure has been followed to establish the functions. The function-1 has been taken for interpretation since its validity and reliability are higher than that of the second function. The estimated discriminant co-efficients are illustrated in Table 4.7.

Table 4.7: Standardised Canonical Discriminant Function Co-efficients

Sl. No.	SQFs	Functions	
		Function–1	Function–2
1.	Reliability	0.9193	0.1717
2.	Responsiveness	0.5027	0.2618
3.	Assurance	0.4163	0.2082
4.	Tangibles	–0.1085	0.3391
5.	Empathy	0.1717	–0.2169
	Per cent of cases correctly classified	91.08	21.03

The function-1 correctly estimates the cases to the extent of 91.08 per cent whereas the function-2 estimates the cases to the extent of 21.03 per cent only. The higher discriminant co-efficients in function-1 are identified in the case of reliability and responsiveness since their co-efficients are 0.9193 and 0.5027 respectively. It indicates that the important discriminators among the three different groups of customers are reliability and responsiveness. The young customers are highly expecting more on these two SQFs than the elders. Hence, the bank managers have to concentrate on these two factors to place the right product/service to the right customer segments.

Gender as a Discriminant of Service Quality Expectation

The gender of the customers can become socialized to behave significantly in their roles as customers. Their nature often overrides behavioural or attitudinal differences attributable to gender (Babin and Roles, 1999).[5] In the management literature, studies have shown that female customers generally expect more than the male customers (Henderson, 1984)[6]. One study found that in male-dominated societies, the female customers were undervalued (Heilman et al., 1989)[7]. Other studies have found stereotypes to be present in occupations, traditionally dominated by one gender (Mackie et al., 1996)[8]. Since the male and female customers are different in the level of expectation, the present study has made an attempt to identify the important discriminant of service quality factors among the male and female customers.

Customers' Expectation on SQFs (Genderwise)

The customers' expectation on SQFs among the male and female customers have been estimated by the mean scores of the expectation on various variables in each factor. The mean scores on expectation among the male and female customers have been analysed to exhibit the level of expectation among them. In order to analyse the significant difference among the male and female customers regarding their level of expectation on SQFs, the 't' test has been administered. The results are given in Table 4.8. (*See Table on next page*)

The total number of male customers selected for the present study is 487 whereas the female customers is 136. The highly expected SQFs among the male customers are assurance and empathy since their respective mean scores are 3.8881 and 3.8142. Among the female customers, the two highly expected SQFs are reliability and empathy since their respective mean scores are 4.4583 and 4.4344. Regarding the level of expectation, the female customers expect more than the male customers but the significant difference among the male and female customers is noticed in their level of expectation on reliability, responsiveness, tangibles and empathy since their respective 't' statistics are significant at five per cent level.

Table 4.8: Customers' Expectation in Service Quality Based on Gender

Sl. No.	SQFs	Mean score among		T-Statistics
		Male	Female	
1.	Reliability	3.5884	4.4583	–2.4508*
2.	Responsiveness	3.6562	4.3039	–2.3991*
3.	Assurance	3.8881	3.9435	–0.2391
4.	Tangibles	3.3039	3.9746	–2.0832*
5.	Empathy	3.8142	4.4344	–1.9983*

* Significant at five per cent level.

Mean Difference and Discriminant Power of SQFs

The discriminant power of SQFs among the male and female customers has been examined with the help of Wilks Lambda. The significant difference among the male and female customers regarding their level of expectation on SQFs have been estimated with the help of its mean difference on SQF expectation and its statistical significance. The results are given in Table 4.9. (*See Table on next page*)

The higher mean differences among the male and female customers have been noticed in reliability, tangibles and responsiveness since their respective mean differences are –0.8699, –0.6707 and –0.6477. The significant mean differences are noticed in the case of reliability, responsiveness, tangibles and empathy since their respective 't' statistics are significant at five per cent level. The higher discriminant power of SQFs is noticed in the case of responsiveness, empathy and reliability since their respective Wilks Lambda are 0.1108, 0.1469 and 0.1971. The significant SQFs have been included for the establishment of the two group discriminant function. The unstandardised procedure has been followed to establish the function. The estimated function is:

$$Z = -0.9661 - 0.2611\ X_1 - 0.1445\ X_2 - 0.1089\ X_4 - 0.4569\ X_5$$

Table 4.9: Mean Difference and Discriminant Power of SQFS (Based on Expectations)

Sl. No.	SQFs	Mean of expectation among		Mean Difference	't' Statistics	Wilks Lambda
		Male	Female			
1.	Reliability	3.5884	4.4583	−0.8699	−2.4508*	0.1971
2.	Responsiveness	3.6562	4.3039	−0.6477	−2.3991*	0.1108
3.	Assurance	3.8881	3.9435	−0.0554	−0.2391	0.5445
4.	Tangibles	3.3039	3.9746	−0.6707	−2.0832*	0.2661
5.	Empathy	3.8142	4.4344	−0.6202	−1.9983*	0.1469

* Significant at five per cent level.

The relative contribution of the service quality factors in the total discriminant score is computed by the product of the discriminant co-efficients and their respective mean difference of the SQFs. The results are given in Table 4.10.

Table 4.10: Relative Contribution of Discriminant SQFS in Total Discriminant Score

Sl. No.	SQFs	Discriminant Co-efficient	Mean Difference	Product	Relative Contribution in TDS
1.	Reliability	−0.2611	−0.8699	0.2271	33.54
2.	Responsiveness	−0.1445	−0.6477	0.0936	13.82
3.	Tangibles	−0.1089	−0.6709	0.0730	10.78
4.	Empathy	−0.4569	−0.6202	0.2834	41.86
	Total			**0.6771**	**100.00**

Per cent of cases correctly classified: 82.96.

The higher discriminant co-efficients are identified in the case of empathy and reliability since their respective discriminant co-efficients are –0.4569 and –0.2611. It reveals the higher degree of influence made by the above said two SQFs on the discriminant function. The higher relative contribution to TDS is noticed in the case of empathy and reliability since the contribution are 41.86 and 33.54 per cent respectively. The analysis reveals that the female customers expect more on empathy and reliability factors than their counterparts. Hence, the service providers consider these factors for the establishment of new product/service strategy to meet the needs of male/female customers.

Level of Education as a Discriminator of Service Quality Expectation

The level of education is one of the important profile variables of the customers. The level of education among the customers has its own influence on the expectation on service quality among the customers in any service industry (Angur,[9] et al., 1999; Anthony and Addams,[10] 2000). The highly educated customers possess more knowledge on the services, service quality and the banking environment in their area (Berry and Parasuraman,[11] 1997). The comparative analysis on service quality offered by the commercial banks is frequently made by the educated customers than the uneducated customers (Joseph and Joseph,[12] 1999). The level of expectation on service quality among the educated and uneducated differ in value added services but not in core services (Jun et al., 1999)[13]. Hence the present analysis focuses on the service quality expectations among the customers with different levels of education and also to identify the important discriminators. The customers are classified into less educated (10th and less than 11th standard), educated (higher secondary and undergraduation level) and highly educated (post-education and professional education).

Customers Expectation on SQFs

The expectation on SQFs among the different education level groups of customers has been analysed to exhibit the level of expectation among the three groups of customers. The mean score of the level of expectation on each SQF is computed by the mean score on the expectation on the variables included in each factor. The oneway analysis of variance has been executed to analyse the significant difference among the three different groups of customers based on their education, regarding their level of expectation on SQFs. The results are given in Table 4.11.

Table 4.11: Expectation on SQFS Among the Different Education Levels of Customers

Sl. No.	SQFs	Mean Scores among			F-Statistics
		Lesser Educated	Educated	Highly Educated	
1.	Reliability	3.1427	3.6861	4.4157	4.2656*
2.	Responsiveness	3.2886	3.8517	4.0898	3.1747*
3.	Assurance	3.7173	3.8682	4.0929	1.9139
4.	Tangibles	3.0456	3.5617	3.5661	3.0969*
5.	Empathy	4.2169	3.9134	3.8094	1.03341

* Significant at five per cent level.

The highly expected SQFs among the lesser educated customers are empathy and assurance since their respective mean scores are 4.2169 and 3.7173 whereas among the educated customers, these are empathy and assurance with the mean score of 3.9134 and 3.8682 respectively. Among the highly educated customers, the highly expected SQFs are reliability and assurance since their respective mean scores are 4.4157 and 4.0929. In total, the level of expectation among the highly educated customers are greater than among others regarding reliability, responsiveness, assurance and tangibles.

The lesser educated customers expect more on empathy. Regarding the expectation, the significant difference among the three different educated groups of customers has been identified in the expectation on reliability, responsiveness and tangibles since their respective 'F' statistics are significant at five per cent level.

Discriminant Service Quality Factors Among the Groups of Educated Customers

Based on education, the customers are classified into three groups namely lesser educated, educated and highly educated. Since, these three groups of customers differ on their nature and exposure, they may be different in their level of expectation on service quality factors. The present analysis has made an attempt to analyse this aspect, with the help of multi discriminant analysis. Initially, the mean of expectation on SQFs among the three groups of customers, its respective 'F' statistics and the Wilks Lambda have been computed and shown in Table 4.12.

Table 4.12: Mean Difference and Discriminant Power of SQFs (Based on Expectations)

Sl. No.	SQFs	Mean of Expectation among Customers who are			F-Statistics	P Value	Wilks Lambda
		Lesser Educated	Educated	Higher Educated			
1.	Reliability	3.1427	3.6861	4.4157	4.2656	0.0144	0.1334
2.	Responsiveness	3.2886	3.8517	4.0898	3.1747	0.0359	0.2161
3.	Assurance	3.7173	3.8682	4.0929	1.9139	0.1096	0.4402
4.	Tangibles	3.0456	3.5617	3.5661	3.0969	0.0461	0.1818
5.	Empathy	4.2169	3.9134	3.8094	1.03341	0.2334	0.5988

The highly educated customers expect more on all SQFs except empathy than the other groups of customers. Regarding the expectation on the SQFs, the significant difference among the three groups of customers has been noticed in the case of expectation on reliability, responsiveness and tangibles since their respective 'F' statistics are significant at five per cent level. The higher discriminant power is identified in the case of reliability and tangibles since their respective Wilks Lambda are 0.1334 and 0.1818 respectively. The analysis reveals that the above said two SQPs are having higher discriminant power to discriminate the three different educated groups of customers.

Canonical Discriminant Function

In order to identify the important discriminant SQFs among the three groups of customers, the multi-discriminant analysis has been executed. Since the number of groups included for the present study is three, the analysis can reveal a maximum of two discriminant functions. Initially, the validity and reliability of these two functions have been examined with the help of its eigen value, per cent of variation explained, canonical correlation and Wilks Lambda. The results are given in Table 4.13. (*See Table on next page*)

The eigen value associated with the first function is 4.3244 and this accounts for 89.09 per cent of the explained variance. Because of the higher value of eigen value, the first function is declared as superior than the second function. The second function has a smaller value of eigen value of 0.3961 and accounts for only 10.92 per cent of the explained variance. The '0' below after function indicates that no functions have been removed. The value of Wilk's Lambda is 0.1433. This transforms to a chi-square of 51.0249, which is significant at zero per cent level. Thus two functions together significantly discriminate the three different educated groups of customers. However, the Wilk's Lambda of the second function is 0.6861, which is not significant at five per cent level. Therefore the second function is declared to be not contributing significantly on group differences.

Table 4.13: Cannonical Discriminant Function

Function	Eigen Value	Per cent of Variance	Cumulative Per cent of Variance	Canonical Correlation	After Function	Wilks Lambda	Chi-Square Value	P Value
1.	4.3244	89.08	89.08	0.8417	0	0.1433	51.0249	0
2.	0.3961	10.92	100.00	0.2161	1	0.6861	2.0961	0.6817

Discriminant Co-efficients of the Various SQFs

In order to identify the important discriminators (expectation) of SQFs among the three different educated groups of customers, the standardized procedure has been followed to establish the two functions. The resultant two functions with their discriminant co-efficients and the per cent of cases correctly estimated by these functions are given in Table 4.14.

Table 4.14: Standardised Canonical Discriminant Function Co-efficients

Sl. No.	SQFs	Functions	
		Function–1	Function–2
1.	Reliability	–0.7142	0.2114
2.	Responsiveness	0.2969	0.3408
3.	Assurance	0.0817	0.0961
4.	Tangibles	0.1445	0.2456
5.	Empathy	0.5142	0.1881
	Per cent of cases correctly classified	87.13	11.45

Since, the first function has more validity and reliability, this function alone has been included for the purpose interpretation. The higher discriminant co-efficients are noticed in the case of reliability and empathy since their co-efficients are 0.7142 and 0.5142 respectively. The results indicates that the important discriminators among the three different educated groups are reliability and empathy. 'Reliability' is highly expected by the highly educated customers whereas 'empathy' is highly expected by the lesser educated customers. Hence, the bank managers should be very careful to design the right product/service to different segment of customers.

Income as a Discriminator of SQF Expectation

The income of the customers is one of the important profile variables of the customers (Lenis, 1991)[14]. The income of the customers have its own influence on their expectation and needs in any service industry (Smith, 1992)[15]. The need and expectations of the higher income class is completely different from the lower income class (Sundaram, 1984)[16]. The higher income class usually expects more on core and value-added services whereas the low income class expects more on core products/services alone (Zeithaml, et al., 1990)[17]. The present analysis has also made an attempt to examine the service quality expectations among the different income groups in order to exhibit the variation in their level of expectation. For this purpose the customers are grouped into Lesser Income Groups (Monthly income Less than Rs. 15,001), Middle Income Groups (Rs. 15,001 to Rs. 25,000) and Higher Income Groups (above Rs. 25,000).

Customers' Expectation on SQFs (Income-wise Analysis)

The customers expectation on the SQFs among different income groups has been estimated by the mean score of the expectation on five SQFs. The score of expectation on SQFs among the customers is computed by the mean scores of the variables in each factor. The oneway analysis of variance has been executed to analyse the significant difference among the three groups of customers in their level of expectation on SQFs. The results are given in Table 4.15. (*See Table on next page*)

The number of customers belonging to LIG, MIG and HIG are 171, 184 and 268 respectively. The highly expected SQFs among the LIG is empathy and assurance since their respective mean scores are 3.9324 and 3.5114. Among the MIG, the highly expected SQFs are assurance and responsiveness since their respective mean scores are 3.8442 and 3.7081 respectively. The highly expected SQFs among the HIG are assurance and reliability since their mean scores are 4.1867 and 4.1426 respectively. Regarding the level of expectation on SQFs, the significant difference among the three groups of customers has been identified in the case of reliability, responsiveness and assurance since their respective 'F' statistics are significant at five per cent level.

Table 4.15: Expectation on SQFS Among the Different Income Groups

Sl. No.	SQFs	Mean scores among			F-Statistics
		Lesser Income Group (LIG)	Middle Income Group (MIG)	Higher Income Group (HIGs)	
1.	Reliability	3.3918	3.6069	4.1426	3.1445*
2.	Responsiveness	3.4602	3.7081	4.0743	3.0424*
3.	Assurance	3.5114	3.8442	4.1867	3.2087*
4.	Tangibles	3.2409	3.3311	3.6658	1.8908
5.	Empathy	3.9324	3.7042	4.1268	0.9965

* Significant at five per cent level.

Discriminant SQFs Among the Three Income Groups

The level of expectation on SQFs among the three income group of customers differ from each other. It is highly essential to identify the level of expectation among the three income groups, the significant difference regarding their level of expectation and the discriminant power of the SQFs to discriminate the three income groups. The mean of the level of expectation on SQFs, their respective 'F' statistics and the Wilks Lambda are summarized in Table 4.16. (*See Table on next page*)

In general, the level of expectation on SQFs is identified to be the highest among the higher income groups than among the other income groups. The significant difference among the three income groups has been noticed in the level of expectation on reliability, responsiveness and assurance since their respective 'F' statistics are significant at five per cent level. The higher discriminant power is noticed in the case of responsiveness and reliability since their respective Wilks Lambda are 0.1081 and 0.1458. These results show that the above said two SQFs have more power to discriminate the three income group customers regarding their level of expectation.

Table 4.16: Mean Difference and Discriminant Power SQFS (Based on Analysis)

Sl. No.	SQFs	Mean of expectation among			F-Statistics	P Value	Wilks Lambda
		LIG	MIG	HIG			
1.	Reliability	3.3918	3.6069	4.1426	3.1445	0.0249	0.1458
2.	Responsiveness	3.4602	3.7081	4.0743	3.0424	0.0355	0.1081
3.	Assurance	3.5114	3.8442	4.1867	3.2087	0.0121	0.2714
4.	Tangibles	3.2409	3.3311	3.6658	1.8908	0.0969	0.3344
5.	Empathy	3.9324	3.7042	4.1268	0.9965	0.1445	0.5646

Canonical Discriminant Function

The influence of the SQFs in the discrimination of the three groups of customers has been examined with the help of Multi Discriminant Analysis. Since the number of groups included for the analysis is only three, the multi discriminant analysis can generate a maximum of only two functions. The reliability and validity of these two functions are analysed with the help of its eigen value, per cent of variance, canonical correlation and Wilks Lambda. The results are given in Table 4.17. (*See Table on next page*)

The eigen value associated with the first function is 4.8563 and this accounts for 86.14 per cent of the explained variance. Because of the high value of eigen value, the first function is declared as superior to the second function. The second function has a smaller eigen value of 0.7939 and accounts for only 13.86 per cent of the explained variance. The '0' below after function indicates that no function has been removed. The value of Wilk's Lambda is 0.1891.

Table 4.17: Canonical Discriminant Function

Function	Eigen Value	Per cent of Variance	Cumulative Per cent of Variance	Canonical Correlation	After Function	Wilks Lambda	Chi-Square Value	P Value
1.	4.8563	86.14	86.14	0.7302	0	0.1891	36.0811	0
2.	0.7939	13.86	100.00	0.2591	1	0.4517	2.1408	0.6339

This transforms to a chi-square of 36.0811, which is significant at zero per cent level. These two functions together significantly discriminate the three income groups. However, the Wilk's Lambda of the second function is 0.4519 which is not significant at five per cent level. Therefore, the second function is not contributing significantly on the group differences.

Discriminant Co-efficients of SQFs

The multi discriminant analysis has been established to identify the discriminant co-efficient of the SQFs. The standardized procedure has been followed to establish the functions. The discriminant co-efficient of the SQFs and their respective per cent of cases correctly classified is shown in Table No. 4.18.

Table 4.18: Standardised Cononical Discriminant Co-efficient

Sl. No.	SQFs	Functions	
		Function-1	Function-2
1.	Reliability	0.8184	0.1241
2.	Responsiveness	0.6071	-0.1097
3.	Assurance	0.5141	0.2616
4.	Tangibles	-0.2049	0.4311
5.	Empathy	-0.1534	0.3317
	Per cent of cases correctly explained	71.09	21.08

Function -1 is taken for the interpretation since its reliability and validity have been proved. The higher discriminant co-efficients are identified in reliability and responsiveness since their respective discriminant co-efficients are 0.8184 and 0.6071. Function-1 estimates the cases correctly to the extent of 71.09 per cent. The analysis reveals that the important discriminant SQFs among the three income groups are reliability and responsiveness. The higher income groups are expecting more on these, compared to the other income groups.

Benefit Segmentation as the Discriminator of Service Quality Expectations

The importance of segmentation in the financial institutional sector has been well documented (Gwin and Lindgran, 1982[18]; Speed and Smith, 1992[19]). As the impact of deregulation on, and proliferation of products within, the financial services sector increased, the need to identify segments to serve became a paramount issue for managers. The challenge of identifying effective segmentation strategies led researchers to a variety of approaches including usage rates for various financial services (Burnelt and Chonoko, 1984)[20], demographics (Burnelt and Wilkes, 1985) [21] and product purchase decisions (Laoche and Taylor, 1988) [22]. One path of segmentation research has been made to pursue determinant attributes analysis of bank selection criteria (Anderson et al., 1976)[23]. While convenience has been a primary determinant in selecting a financial institution, Anderson et al., (1976) identified two distinct segments namely, the convenience-oriented group and the service-oriented group. Subsequent research has suggested other determinant attributes, depending on the orientation (e.g. sophistication, ambience) of the customers (Kinnacid et al., 1984) [24]. The value of this approach is that it attempts to understand the primary benefits that customers are seeking from a financial institution. The present study has been made an attempt to analyse the level of expectation on SQFs among the two different benefit seekers namely convenience and performance seekers. The study also tries to establish the important SQFs which discriminate the above said two groups of customers regarding their level of expectation. The results are given in Table 4.19.

Customers' Expectation on SQFs

The level of expectation on SQFs among the convenience and performance seekers has been computed from the mean scores of expectation on SQFs in commercial banks. The score of expectation on SQFs is derived from the mean score of the variables in each factor. The one way analysis of variance has been executed to find out the significant difference among the two types of customers. The results are shown in Table 4.19.

Table 4.19: Expectation on SQFS Among the Convenience and Performance Seekers

Sl. No.	SQFs	Mean score among		'T' Statistics
		Convenience Seekers (CSs)	Performance Seekers (PSs)	
1.	Reliability	3.3646	3.9083	-2.0457*
2.	Responsiveness	3.1142	4.0124	-2.8343*
3.	Assurance	3.4505	4.0412	-2.1142*
4.	Tangibles	3.6818	3.3775	1.5033
5.	Empathy	4.2165	3.8656	1.7417

* Significant at five per cent level.

The highly expected SQF among the convenience seekers is empathy since its mean score is 4.2165 whereas among the performance seekers, these are assurance and responsiveness since their respective mean scores are 4.0412 and 4.0124. Regarding the level of expectation, the significant difference among the convenience and performance seekers have been identified in the expectation on reliability, responsiveness and assurance since their respective 't' statistics are significant at five per cent level. The convenience seekers expect more on tangibles and empathy whereas the performance seekers expect more on reliability, responsiveness and assurance.

Level of Expectation on SQFs

The level of expectation on SQFs among the convenience and performance seekers has been analysed with the help of the mean scores of the level of expectation on five SQFs among the two groups of customers. The 't' test has been administered to find out the significant mean difference among the two groups of customers regarding their mean difference in each SQFs. The discriminant power of the SQFs have been estimated with the help of Wilk's Lambda. The results are given in Table 4.20.

Table 4.20: Mean Difference and Discriminant Power of SQFS Among Convenience and Performance Seekers

Sl. No.	SQFs	Mean of expectation among		Mean Difference	t-Statistics	Wilk's Lambda
		Convenience seekers	Performance seekers			
1.	Reliability	3.3646	3.9083	-0.5437	-2.0457*	0.2103
2.	Responsiveness	3.1142	4.0124	-0.8982	-2.8343*	0.1248
3.	Assurance	3.4505	4.0412	-0.5907	-2.1142*	0.1819
4.	Tangibles	3.6818	3.3775	0.3043	1.5033	0.3392
5.	Empathy	4.2165	3.8656	0.3509	1.7417	0.1458

* Significant at five per cent level.

The significant mean different among the convenience and performance seekers have been noticed in the case of reliability, responsiveness and assurance since their respective 't' statistics are significant at five per cent level. The higher mean difference is identified in the case of responsiveness and assurance since their respective mean differences are -0.8982 and -0.5907. The higher discriminant power is identified in responsiveness and empathy since their respective Wilks Lambda are 0.1248 and 0.1458. The significant SQFs have been included to estimate the two groups' discriminant function. The unstandardised procedure has been followed to estimate the functions. The estimated two group procedure function is

$$Z = -1.2396 - 0.8517x_1 - 0.4042x_2 - 0.3391\, x_3$$

The relative contribution of discriminant SQFs in total discriminant score is estimated by the product of the discriminant co-efficients and the respective mean difference of the SQFs. The results are presented in Table 4.21.

Table 4.21: Relative Contribution of Discriminant SQFS in Total Discriminant Score (TDS)

Sl. No.	SQFs	Discriminant Co-efficient	Mean Difference	Product	Relative Contribution of SQFs in TDS (in %)
1.	Reliability	-0.8517	-0.5437	0.4631	45.11
2.	Responsiveness	-0.4042	-0.8982	0.3631	35.37
3.	Assurance	-0.3391	-0.5907	0.2003	19.52
	Total			**1.0265**	**100.00**

Per cent of cases correctly classified: 79.11.

The higher discriminant co-efficient is identified in the case of reliability since its co-efficient is -0.8517. It infers that the above said SQF has more influence on the discriminant function. The higher relative contribution of SQF in TDS, is noticed in the case of reliability and responsiveness since their respective contributes are 45.11 and 35.37 per cent to their respective total. The estimated discriminant function correctly classifies the cases to the extent of 79.11 per cent. The analysis reveals that the important discriminant SQFs among the convenience and performance seekers are reliability and responsiveness.

Occupation as the Discriminator of Service Quality Expectation

The occupation among the customers reveals the nature of business or work done by the customers. Since 'occupation' is one of the importance profile variables which will lead to the expectation of various services in the banking industry (Albrecht and Zembe, 1985[25]; Bolton and Drew, 1991[26]), it is included as one of the demographic variables in the present study. Based on occupation, the customers are classified into agriculturalists, employees and businessmen. The level of expectation on SQFs among the three groups of customers, has been computed by the mean of expectation on five SQFs. The one-way analysis has been executed to analyse the significant difference among the three groups of customers.

The agriculturalists include the customers whose occupation is agriculture and agriculture allied activities. The term 'employees' covers the customers working in Government and Private sectors. The 'businessmen' includes the customers who are businessmen and professionals. In total, the number of customers who are agriculturist, employees and businessmen constitute 26, 32.10 and 41.90 per cent to their respective total. The expectation of SQFs among the three occupational groups of customers has been computed and illustrated in Table 4.22.

Table 4.22: Expectation on SQFS Among the Customers Based on Occupation

Sl. No.	SQFs	Mean Scores among			F-Statistics
		Agriculturalist	Employees	Businessmen	
1.	Reliability	3.4468	3.6177	4.1071	2.8188*
2.	Responsiveness	3.5212	3.6224	4.1034	2.0334
3.	Assurance	3.3446	3.8917	4.2516	3.1786*
4.	Tangibles	3.0642	3.3344	3.7788	3.0441*
5.	Empathy	3.6187	3.5946	4.4270	3.3892*

* Significant at five per cent level.

The highly expected SQFs among the agriculturalists are empathy and responsiveness since their respective mean scores are 3.6187 and 3.5212 whereas among the employees, these two variables are assurance and responsiveness since their mean scores are 3.8917 and 3.6224 respectively. Among the businessmen, the highly expected SQFs are empathy and assurance since their mean of level of expectations are 4.4270 and 4.2516 respectively. Regarding the level of expectation, the significant difference among the three occupational groups of customers has been identified in the case of expectation on reliability, assurance, tangibles and empathy since their respective 'F' statistics are significant at five per cent level.

Mean Difference and Discriminant Power of SQFs among the Three Occupational Groups of Customers

The customers belonging to the three different groups based on their occupation, may be different in their level of expectation. The bank managers have to understand the level of expectation among them and also analyse the discriminant power of SQFs among them. In the present analysis, an attempt has been made to analyse the significant difference among the three groups of customers with the help of one-way analysis of variance. The discriminant power of the SQFs has been estimated with the help of Wilks Lambda. The results are given in Table 4.23. (*See Table on next page*)

The significant difference among the three groups of customers, regarding their level of expectation on SQFs has been noticed in the case of expectation on reliability, assurance, tangibles and empathy since their respective 'F' statistics are significant at five per cent level. In general, the businessmen are expecting more on SQFs compared to the other two groups of customers. The higher discriminant power of the SQFs is identified in the case of empathy, assurance and reliability since their respective Wilk's Lambda are 0.1219, 0.1346 and 0.1843. It reveals that the above said three SQFs have more power to discriminate the three groups of customers.

Table 4.23: Mean Difference and Discriminant Power of SQFs (Based on Expectations)

Sl. No.	SQFs	Mean of Expectation among			F-Statistics	P Value	Wilks Lambda
		Agriculturalist	Employees	Businessmen			
1.	Reliability	3.4468	3.6177	4.1071	2.8188	0.0501	0.1843
2.	Responsiveness	3.5212	3.6224	4.1034	2.0334	0.1618	0.4661
3.	Assurance	3.3446	3.8917	4.2516	3.1786	0.0259	0.1346
4.	Tangibles	3.0642	3.3344	3.7788	3.0441	0.0339	0.2214
5.	Empathy	3.6187	3.5946	4.4270	3.3892	0.0186	0.1219

Canonical Discriminant Function

The relative importance of the SQFs in discriminating the three groups of customers (based on occupation) has been analysed with the help of multi discriminant analysis. The scores of expectation on various SQFs, among the three occupational groups of customers have been included for the analysis. Since, the present study includes only three groups of customers, the multi discriminant analysis can generate two functions. The validity and reliability of these two functions are tested with the help of eigen value, per cent of variance, canonical correlation and Wilk's Lambda. The results are given in Table 4.24. (*See Table on next page*)

The eigen value and the per cent of variance explained by the first function are 6.0917 and 91.31 per cent respectively. Since these two values are very high, the first function is declared as superior than the function-2. It is also supported by the canonical correlation of the function-1 which is 0.8549. The second function has a smaller eigen value of 0.7334 and accounts for only 8.69 per cent of the explained variance. The '0' below after function indicates that no function has been removed. The value of Wilk's Lambda is 0.1208. This transforms to a chi-square of 55.6162, which is significant at five per cent level. These two functions, together, significantly discriminate the three occupational groups. However, the Wilk's Lambda of the second function is 0.8646 which is not significant at the five per cent level. Therefore, the second function is declared to be not contributing significantly on the group differences.

Discriminant Co-efficients of SQFs

The multi discriminant analysis has been established to identify the discriminant co-efficients of the SQFs. The standardized procedure has been followed to establish the functions. The discriminant co-efficient of the SQFs and their respective per cent of cases correctly classified is shown in Table 4.25. (*See Table on page 121*)

Table 4.24: Cannonical Discriminant Function

Function	Eigen Value	Per cent of Variance	Cumulative Per cent of Variance	Canonical Correlation	After Function	Wilks Lambda	Chi-square Value	P Value
1.	6.0917	91.31	91.31	0.8549	0	0.1208	55.6162	0.0000
2.	0.7334	8.69	100.00	0.2611	1	0.8646	2.1704	0.5686

Table 4.25: Standardised Canonical Discriminant Function Co-efficient

Sl. No.	SQFs	Functions	
		Function-1	Function-2
1.	Reliability	-0.8649	0.0821
2.	Responsiveness	0.5081	-0.3144
3.	Assurance	-0.2162	0.4569
4.	Tangibles	0.1819	0.1334
5.	Empathy	-1.2144	0.2145
	Per cent of cases correctly classified	91.29	15.69

The function-1 is taken for the interpretation since its validity and reliability have been proved. The higher discriminant co-efficients are identified in the case of empathy and reliability since their respective discriminant co-efficients are -0.2144 and 0.8649. Function-1 estimates the cases correctly to the extent of 91.29 per cent. The analysis reveals that the important discriminant SQFs among the three occupational groups are empathy and reliability. The empathy and reliability are expected more by the businessmen than the other two groups of customers.

Banking Experience as a Discriminant of Service Quality Expectations

Effective segmentation is a challenge for financial service managers. It investigates the use of service quality, years of experience and competitiveness as a basis for customers segment (Gordon et al., 1994)[27]. Years of experience in banking among the customers has also been a popular demographic variable utilized by a myriad of product and service marketers. The experience segmentation does not automatically assume targeting those having higher experience. The levels of expectation on SQFs among the experienced and lesser experienced customers are different

(Parasuraman et al., 1991[28]; Speed and Smith, 1992[29]; Hood and Walters, 1985[30]). Usually, the experienced customers expect more from their service providers. Their expectations are also growing since they are comparing the services offered by other service providers. But it is not so in the case of less experienced customers (Galiano and Hath Cote, 1994)[31]. In the present study, an attempt has been made to analyse the level of expectation among customers with different experience and also to identify the discriminant SQFs among them.

Customers' Expectation on SQFs Among different Experienced Groups of Customers

Out of 623 customers included for the present study, the number of customers who are less experienced, experienced and highly experienced are 118, 261 and 234 customers respectively. The expectation on SQFs among the three groups has been estimated by the mean score of expectation on SQFs. The score of expectation on SQFs is derived from the mean score of the expectation on the variables in each SQF. The one-way analysis of variance has been executed to find out the significant difference among the three groups of customers regarding their level of expectation.

Table 4.26: Expectation on SQFS Among the Different Experienced Customers

Sl. No.	SQFs	Mean scores among			F-Statistics
		Less Experienced	Experienced	Highly Experienced	
1.	Reliability	3.4561	3.6121	4.1118	3.1089*
2.	Responsiveness	3.4802	3.5089	4.2598	3.3646*
3.	Assurance	3.6119	3.6343	4.3240	3.2108*
4.	Tangibles	3.2081	3.3241	3.7024	2.9111*
5.	Empathy	3.5141	3.7028	4.4242	3.4503*

* Significant at five per cent level.

The highly expected SQFs among the less experienced customers are assurance and empathy since their mean scores are 3.6119 and 3.5141 respectively. Among the experienced customers, these are empathy and assurance since their mean scores are 3.7028 and 3.6343 respectively. The highly expected SQFs among the highly experienced customers are empathy and assurance since their respective mean scores are 4.4242 and 4.3240. Regarding the level of expectation on SQFs, the significant difference among the three groups of customers has been noticed in the expectation on all five SQFs since their respective 'F' statistics are significant at five per cent level.

Mean Difference and Discriminant Power of SQFs

The level of service quality expectations on SQFs among the Less Experienced Group (LED), Experienced (ED) and Higher Experienced Group (HED) have been analysed with the help of their mean scores of the expectation on five SQFs and their significance difference. The one-way analysis of variance has been executed to find out the significant difference. The discriminant power of the SQFs has been estimated with the help of its Wilk's Lambda. The resultant mean of expectation score on each SQF, its 'F' statistics, p-value and the Wilk's Lambda is presented in Table 4.27.

Table 4.27: Mean Difference and Discriminant Power SQFS (Based on Expectations)

Sl. No.	SQFs	Mean of expectation among			F-Statistics	P Value	Wilk's Lambda
		LED	ED	HED			
1.	Reliability	3.4561	3.6121	4.1118	3.1089	0.0311	0.2604
2.	Responsiveness	3.4802	3.5089	4.2598	3.3646	0.0197	0.1317
3.	Assurance	3.6119	3.6343	4.3240	3.2108	0.0268	0.1813
4.	Tangibles	3.2081	3.3241	3.7024	2.9111	0.0417	0.3776
5.	Empathy	3.5141	3.7028	4.4242	3.4503	0.0145	0.2961

The significant difference among the three groups of customers has been identified in their expectation on reliability, responsiveness, assurance, tangibles and empathy since their respective 't' statistics are significant at five per cent level. The lower level Wilk's Lambda has been noticed in the case of responsiveness and assurance since their Wilk's Lambda are 0.1317 and 0.1813 respectively. It reveals that the above said two SQFs have more discriminant power to discriminant the different customers.

Canonical Discriminant Function

The discriminant function has been established with the help of multi discriminant analysis. Since there are three experienced groups in the present study, the multi discriminant analysis can generate two functions. The reliability and validity of these functions have been computed. The computed validity and reliability measures of the two functions are given in Table No. 4.28. (*See Table on next page*)

The eigen value associated with the first function is 4.3969 and this accounts for 91.08 per cent of the explained variance. Because of the high eigen value, the first function is declared as superior than the second function. The second function has a smaller value of eigen value of 0.5641 and accounts for only 8.92 per cent of explained variance. The '0' below after function indicates that no function has been removed. The value of Wilk's Lambda is 0.1027. This transforms to a chi-square of 61.2392 which is significant at zero per cent level. Thus the two functions together significantly discriminate the three different experienced groups of customers. However, the Wilk's Lambda of the second function is 0.7336, which is not significant at five per cent level. Therefore, the second function is declared to be not contributing significantly on group differences.

Discriminant Co-efficient of the SQFs

The relative importance of the SQFs in the discriminant function has been computed with the help of the discriminant

Table 4.28: Cannonical Discriminant Function

Function	Eigen Value	Per cent of Variance	Cumulative Per cent of Variance	Canonical Correlation	After Function	Wilks Lambda	Chi-square Value	P Value
1.	4.3969	91.08	91.08	0.8917	0	0.1027	61.2392	0.0000
2.	0.5641	8.92	100.00	0.1339	1	0.7336	2.4503	0.7139

function. The standardized procedure has been followed to establish such discriminant function. Since, Function-1 have been declared as superior than Function-2, the discriminant co-efficients of SQFs in Function-1 alone have been taken for further interpretation. The standardized canonical discriminant co-efficients of the SQFs in Function-1 and Function-2 are given in Table 4.29.

Table 4.29: Standardised Canonical Discriminant Function Co-efficient

Sl. No.	SQFs	Functions	
		Function-1	Function-2
1.	Reliability	0.2145	0.5168
2.	Responsiveness	-0.4509	0.2041
3.	Assurance	-0.8617	-0.1334
4.	Tangibles	0.1776	0.1291
5.	Empathy	0.3314	0.2608
	Per cent of cases correctly classified	89.17	20.08

Function-1 reveals that the important discriminant SQFs among the three groups of customers are assurance and responsiveness since their respective discriminant co-efficients are -0.8617 and -0.4509. The estimated function-1 classifies the cases correctly to the extent of 89.17 per cent. The analysis reveals that the experienced and less experienced customers are highly discriminated by their level of expectation on assurance and responsiveness. The highly experienced customers are expecting more on the above said two SQFs compared to the other two groups of customers.

REFERENCES

1. Bernett, D., and Higgins, M., (1988), "Quality Means More than Smiles", *ABA Banking Journal*, June, p. 6.

2. Bowen, J.W. and Hedges, R.B., (1993), "Increasing service quality in retail banking", *Journal of Retail Banking*, 15 (1), pp. 21-28.

3. Gagliano, K.B. and Itathcote, J., (1994), "Customer Expectation and Perceptions of Service Quality in Retail Apparel Speciality Stores", *Journal of Service Marketing*, 8(1), pp. 60-69.

4. Webster, C. (1989), "Can Consumers be Segmented on the Basis of Their Service Quality Expectations?", *Journal of Service Marketing*, 3(2), pp. 35-53.

5. Babin, B.J., and Boles, J.S., (1998), "Customer Behaviour in a Service Environment: A Model and Test of Potential Difference between Men and Women", *Journal of Marketing*, 62 (April), pp. 71-91.

6. Henderson, R.I., (1984), *Performance Appraisal*, Reston Publishing Co., Reston, VA.

7. Heilman, M.E., Martell, R.F. and Simon, M.C., (1989), "The Vagaries of Sex Bias: Conditions Regulating the Undervaluation, Equivaluation and Overvaluation of Female Job Applicants", Organ Behaviour and Human Decision Proc., Vol. 41, pp. 98-110.

8. Mackie, D., Hamilton, D., Susskind, J., and Rosselli, F., (1996), "Social Psychological Foundations of Stereotype Formation", Macrae, C.N., Stangor, C. and Hewstone, M., *Stereotypes and Stereotyping*, The Guilford Press, New York, NY.

9. Angur, M.G., Natarajan, R. and Jahera, J.S., (1999), "Service Quality in the Banking Industry: An Assessment in a Developing Economy", *International Journal of Bank Marketing*, 17(3), pp. 116-123.

10. Anthony, T.A. and Addams, H.I., (2000), "Service Quality at Banks and Credit Unions: What do Their Customers Say?", *Managing Service Quality*, 10(1), pp. 52-60.

11. Berry, L.C. and Parasuraman, A., (1997), "Listening to the Customers – The Concept of A Service Quality Information System", *Gloan Management Review*, Spring, pp. 65-76.

12. Joseph, M., McClure, C. and Joseph, B., (1999), "Service Quality in the Banking Sector: The Impact of Technology on Service Delivery", *International Journal of Bank Marketing*, 17(4), pp. 182-191.

13. Jun, M., Peterson, R.J., Zsidison, G.A., and Daily, B.F., (1999), "Service Quality Perceptions in the Banking Industry – Major Dimensions", *Journal of Business Strategies*, 16 (2), pp.170-188.

14. Lenis, B., (1991), "Service quality: An International Companion of Bank Customers' Expectations and Perceptions", *Journal of Marketing Management*, 7(1), pp. 47-62.

15. Smith, A.M., (1992), "The Consumers' Evaluation of Service Quality: Some Methodological Issues" in Glynon, W.J., and Barnes, J.P., (1995) *Understanding Service Management*, (eds.) New York, John Wiley and Sons, pp. 57-88.

16. Sundaram, S., (1984), "Customer Service in Banks at Cross Roads", *The Journal of the Indian Institute of Bankers*, 55 (4), pp. 217-223.

17. Zeithaml, V.A., Parasuraman, A., Berry, L.C., (1990), "Delivering Quality Services: Balancing Customer Perception and Expectations", New York, Free Press, p. 28.

18. Gwin, J.M., Lindgren, J.H., (1982), "Banking on established customer", *Journal of Retail Banking*, 4(4), pp. 8-13.

19. Speed, R. and Smith, G., (1992), "Retail Financial Services Segmentation", The Service Industrial Journal, 12(3), pp. 368-383.

20. Burnelt, J.J., Chonko, L.B., (1984), "A Segmental Approach to Packing Bank Products", *Journal of Retail Banking*, 6(2), pp. 37-48.

21. Burnelt, J.J. and Wilkes, R.E., (1985), "An Appraisal of the senior citizens market segment", *Journal of Retail Banking*, 7(4), pp. 57-64.

22. Lawche, M. and Taylor, T., (1988), "An empirical study of major segmentation issues in Retail Banking", *International Journal of Bank Marketing*, 6(1), pp. 31-48.

23. Anderson, W.T., Cox, X.P., III and Fulcher, D.H. (1976), "Bank Selection Decisions and Market Segmentation", *Journal of Marketing*, 40(1), pp. 40-45.

24. Kinnaird, D., Shaughnessy, K., Struman, K.D., Sinnyar, W.R., (1984), "Market Segmentation of Retail Bank Services: A Model for Management", Journal of Retail Banking, 6(3), pp. 53-63.

25. Albrecht, K., and Zemke, R., (1985), "Service America: Doing Business in the New York in Lewis, Bartara, (1991), "Service Quality: An International Comparison of Bank Customer Expectation and Perceptives", *Journal of Marketing Management*, 7(1), pp. 47-62.

26. Bolton, R.N., and Drew, J.H. (1991), "A Multi Stage Model of Customer's Assessment of Service quality and value", *Journal of Consumer Research*, 17(4), pp. 375-384.

27. Gordon, H.G., Mc.Dongall, Terrence, J. Levesqur, (1994), "Benefit Segmentation using Service quality Dimensions – An Investigation in Retail Banking", *International Journal of Bank Marketing*, 12(2), pp. 15-23.

28. Parasuraman, A., Berry, L.L. and Zeithaml, V.A., (1991), "Understanding Consumers' Expectations of Service", Sloan Management Review, *Spring*, pp. 39-48.

29. Speed, R. and Smith, G., (1992), "Retail Financial Services Segmentation", *The Service Industries Journal*, 12(3), pp. 368-383.

30. Hood, J.M., and Walkers, C.G., (1985), "Banking on established Customers", *Journal of Retail Banking*, 7(1), pp. 35-40.

31. Gagliamo, Kathryn, B., and Jan Hathcote (1994), "Customer Expectations and Perceptions of Service quality in Retail Appraisal Speciality stress", *Journal of Service Marketing*, 8(1), pp. 60-139.

Customers Segmentation Analysis

The commercial banks competing with each other in the market, with generally undifferentiated products, service quality becomes a primary competitive weapon. Recently, this area is focused by more market researchers since the reduced customer base and decreased market share affect a portion of banking industry (Bowen and Headges, 1993)[1]. They also advocated to select the most important customers in order to satisfy since it is very difficult to satisfy all customer segments simultaneously with a uniform service and service quality. The primary question that arises before the researcher is "who are the customers" and "what do they want?" Both the questions are completely influenced by the demographic profile of the customers. Hence, it is essential to identify the role of demographic variables in the expectation and perception on various SQFs in commercial banks. It is equally important to identify the important discrimators of SQFs among the different groups of customers, based on each profile.

Demography continues to be one of the most popular and well accepted bases for segmenting markets and customers (Belch and Belch, 1993[2]; Kotler and Armstrong, 1991[3]). By specifically identifying the key demography of one's target market, a basic profile of the targeted customer emerges. Even if other types of segmentation variables are used (e.g., behavioural, psychographic) a marketer must know and understand demography to assess the size, reach and efficiency of the market (Kotler and Armstrong, 1991). Lazer (1994) pointed out the importance of demographics and their relationship with marketing. In the present study, an attempt has been made on the SERVQUAL and SERVPER scale on the SQFs among the different groups of customers based on each demographic profile. Even though, the profile variables are too many, the present study is confined to nativity (Urban and Rural), age (Youngsters, Middle aged and Aged), gender (Male and Female), level of education (Less Educated, Educated and Highly Educated), income (Less Income Group, Middle Income Group and Higher Income Group), benefit seekers (Convenience seekers and performance seekers), occupation (Agriculturalists, Employees and Businessmen) and years of experience (Less experienced, Experienced and Highly experienced).

Service Quality of Commercial Banks: Perspective of Urban and Rural Customers

One of the important profiles of the customers is their 'Nativity' i.e urban and rural customers. The level of expectation and perception on the SQFs of commercial banks among the two groups of customers differ from each other. The urban customer's requirements and expectation from the commercial banks are related to his environment. Usually, the urban customers have more knowledge on banking products and services and also about the competitive services offered by other commercial banks. Among the rural customers, it is comparatively less but slowly growing. The need and expectations among them are different. In the competitive environment, there is vast scope of unstopped market in rural India even in commercial banking. Hence, it is essential to identify the level of perception on SQFs among the two groups of customers and also to identify the discriminate SQFs among the two groups for future policy implication.

SERVPERF Scale on SQFs

The customers' perceptions on the SQFs in commercial banks are also measured by the mean score of the perception on variables in each factor. The mean scores of perception on SQFs have been computed to exhibit the level of perception on SQFs among the urban and rural customers. Regarding the level of perception among the two groups of customers, the 't' test has been administered. The resultant mean scores of perception on five SQFs and their respective 't' statistics are illustrated in Table 5.1.

Table 5.1: Customers' Perception on Service Quality Factors (SERVPERF Scale)

Sl. No.	Service Quality Factors	Mean Score among Customers in		'T'-statistics
		Urban	Rural	
1.	Reliability	3.4568	2.3489	3.6817*
2.	Responsiveness	3.3692	2.6923	3.4591*
3.	Assurance	3.2106	2.8329	1.0965
4.	Tangibles	3.1091	2.4874	1.4861
5.	Empathy	3.5043	2.2814	3.5909*

* Significant at five per cent level

By the level of perception on SQFs, as seen from the above table the urban customers are rating all five SQFs in a better manner than the rural customers. The highly perceived SQFs among the urban customers are empathy and reliability since their respective mean scores are 3.5043 and 3.4568. Among the rural customers, these two SQFs are assurance and responsiveness since their respective mean scores are 2.8329 and 2.6923. Regarding the level of perception, the significant difference among the urban and rural customers has been identified in the perception on reliability, responsiveness and empathy since their respective 't' statistics are significant at five per cent level.

SERVQUAL scale on SQFs

The SERVQUAL scale indicates the difference between the level of perception and expectation on each SQF in commercial banks among the customers. The SERVQUAL scale on SQFs among the urban and rural customers has been computed to exhibit the level of deviation between these two levels among the two groups of customers. The negative SERVQUAL scale requires the immediate attention on these areas by the bank managers since the customers are not satisfied upto their level of expectation. The significant difference among the two groups of customers regarding all five SQFs has been computed with the help of 't' test.

Table 5.2: SERVQUAL Scale Among the Customers

Sl. No.	Service Quality Factors	Mean Score among Customers		'T'-statistics
		Urban	Rural	
1.	Reliability	-0.4746	-0.5992	-0.4508
2.	Responsiveness	-0.5411	-0.4941	0.3811
3.	Assurance	-0.8763	-0.0548	2.1176*
4.	Tangibles	-0.5822	0.3435	1.9813*
5.	Empathy	-0.7045	-0.2626	2.0441*

* Significant at five per cent level.

Table 5.2 explains the mean scores of SERVQUAL scale on all five SQFs and their respective 't' statistics. The result indicates that all SERVQUAL scores are negative. It reveals that the level of perception related to the level of expectation on all five SQFs among the two groups of customers is less.

Higher SERVQUAL scale is identified in the case of assurance and empathy since their mean scores are -0.8763 and -0.7045 respectively. Among the rural customers, it is noticed in the case of reliability and responsiveness since their mean scores are -0.5992 and -0.4941 respectively. Regarding the SERVQUAL scale, significant difference among the urban and rural customers has been noticed in the case of assurance, tangibles and empathy since their respective 't' statistics are significant at five per cent level.

Customers' Satisfaction Index Among the Customers

The customer satisfaction has been measured with the help of an index called 'Customer Satisfaction Index' (CSI). It reveals the summative view of the customers' satisfaction towards the various aspects related to banking. The CSI in the present study is confined to less than 21 per cent, 21 to 40, 41 to 60, 61 to 80 and above 80 per cent. The distribution of customers on the basis of CSI is given in Table 5.3.

Table 5.3: Customers Satisfaction Index (CSI) Among the Customers

Sl. No.	CSI (in per cent)	Number of Customers		Total
		Urban	Rural	
1.	Less than 21	65	14	79
2.	21- 40	127	21	148
3.	41- 60	174	30	204
4.	61- 80	88	17	105
5.	Above 80	72	15	87
	Total	**526**	**97**	**623**

The important CSI among the customers are 41 to 60 and 21 to 40 per cent which constitute 32.74 and 23.75 per cent to their respective total. The number of customers with the CSI of less than 21 per cent constitutes 12.68 per cent of the total. The important CSI among the urban customers are

41 to 60 per cent and 21 to 40 per cent which constitute 33.08 and 24.14 per cent to their respective total. Among the rural customers, these two are 41 to 60 per cent and 21 to 40 per cent which constitute 30.93 and 21.65 per cent to their respective total. Regarding customers satisfaction, the rural customers are slightly more satisfied than the urban customers.

Impact of SERVPERF Scale of SQF on CSI

The perception on SQFs among the customers may have its own impact on customer satisfaction. It is highly imperative to identify the impact of each SQF on the CSI for some policy implications. The multiple regression analysis has been executed to find out such impact. The ordinary least square method is followed to fit the multiple regression model. The resultant regression coefficients of the SQFs are given in Table 5.4.

Table 5.4: Impact of SERVPERF Scale of SQFS on CSI

Sl. No.	SQFs	Regression coefficient among customers	
		Urban	Rural
1.	Reliability	0.3109*	0.1461*
2.	Responsiveness	0.2411*	0.2201*
3.	Assurance	0.1002	0.0968
4.	Tangibles	0.0917	0.1947*
5.	Empathy	0.1861*	0.2868*
	Constant	0.5687	1.2146
	R^2	0.7339	0.6861
	F-Statistics	11.2308*	9.3091*

* Significant at five per cent level.

The SQFs significantly influencing on customers satisfaction among the urban customers are reliability, responsiveness and empathy since their respective regression coefficients are significant at five per cent level. A unit increase in the perception on the above said SQFs would result in an increase in customer satisfaction by 0.3019, 0.2411 and 0.1861 units respectively. The changes in the perception on SQFs explain the changes in customer satisfaction index to the extent of 73.39 per cent since their respective R^2 is 0.7339.

Among the rural customers, the significantly influencing perception on SQFs are reliability, responsiveness, tangibles and empathy. A unit increase in the perception on the above said SQFs would result in an increase in CSI by 0.1461, 0.2201, 0.1947 and 0.2868 units respectively. The changes in the perception on SQFs explain the changes in CSI to the extent of 68.61 per cent only. The analysis reveals that the most significantly influencing SQFs on the customer satisfaction among the urban and rural customers are reliability and empathy respectively.

Discriminate SQF Among the Urban and Rural Customers

In order to formulate a suitable marketing strategy, the policy makers have to identify the important discriminate SQFs among the urban and rural customers. It reveals the SQFs which discriminate the two groups. The perception score on all five SQFs have been included for the two group discriminate analysis. The unstandardized procedure has been followed to establish the discriminate function. Initially, the mean difference of each SQF and its statistical significance have been analysed. The discriminate power of the SQFs is examined with the help of Wilk's Lambda. The results are given in Table 5.5. (*See Table on next page*)

Out of five SQFs, the significant mean difference among the urban and rural customers has been noticed in the case of reliability, responsiveness and empathy since their respective 't' statistics are significant at five per cent level. The higher discriminate power of SQFs is identified in the case of reliability and empathy since their respective Wilk's

Lambda are 0.1208 and 0.1644. The significant SQFs have been included to establish the two group discriminate function. The established function is

$$Z = 0.8969+0.2139X_1+0.3632X_2+0.1778X_5$$

Table 5.5: Mean Difference and the Discriminate Power of the SQFS

Sl. No.	SQFs	Mean score among customers		'T' statistics	P-Value	Wilk's Lambda
		Urban	Rural			
1.	Reliability	3.4568	2.3489	3.6817	0.0039	0.1208
2.	Responsiveness	3.3692	2.6923	3.4591	0.0145	0.2104
3.	Assurance	3.2106	2.8329	1.0965	0.2608	0.5409
4.	Tangibles	3.1091	2.4874	1.4861	0.1349	0.2683
5.	Empathy	3.5043	2.2814	3.5909	0.0091	0.1644

The relative contribution of each SQF in total discriminate score is computed by the product of the unstandardized canonical discriminate coefficient of the SQF and its respective mean difference. The computed discriminate coefficients and the relative contribution of SQFs in total discriminate score is explained in Table 5.6. (*See Table on next page*)

The higher discriminate coefficient is identified in responsiveness since its coefficient is 0.3632. It infers that the degree of influence of responsiveness on the two group discriminate function is very high compared to the other SQFs. It is followed by reliability. The higher contribution of SQFs in total discriminate score is also identified in the case of responsiveness and reliability since their respective relative contributions are 35.12 and 33.83 per cent respectively. The estimated two group discriminate function correctly classifies the cases to the extent of 69.77 per cent. The analysis reveals that the urban and rural customers are discriminated mainly by the SQFs namely reliability, responsiveness and empathy. The urban customers are expecting and perceiving more on the above said three SQFs than the rural customers.

Table 5.6: Relative Contribution of Significant SQFS in Total Discriminate Score (TDS)

Sl. No.	SQFs	Unstandardized canonical discriminate coefficient	Mean Difference	Product	Relative contribution in TDS (in per cent)
1.	Reliability	0.2139	1.1079	0.2369	33.83
2.	Responsiveness	0.3632	0.6769	0.2459	35.12
3.	Empathy	0.1778	1.2229	0.2174	31.05
	Total			**0.7002**	**100.00**

Per cent of cases correctly classified: 69.77

Age-Wise Segmentation Analysis

The age of the customers is one of the important profiles of the customers. Even though the younger customers are usually having less experience with the banking activities, they are very eager to know the latest development in the banking industry. They try to compare the services offered by their bank with the other banks. Usually, the youngsters may not be loyal to the existing bank since they are benefit seekers. They never hesitate to switch over to other banks which are providing better service. At the same time, the elders are not traditionalists. They are highly experienced. Hence their perception on the SQFs may reveal the correct picture on the service quality of the commercial banks. The elderly people may be easily attached with the existing bank and they hesitate to switch over to other banks because of the expenses involved in switching over and also their loyalty towards the bank. In the present competitive scenario, the bank marketers have to retain the existing customers since the cost of acquiring new customers is higher than the cost of retaining the existing customers. Hence, they have to deliver customized service. For this they have to know the level of expectation and perception on various SQFs among the customers belonging to different age groups. In the present study, the customers are classified into youngsters (less than 36 years), middle aged (36 to 55 years) and aged (above 55 years).

Customers' Perception on SQFs Among Different Age Groups

The perception on the five SQFs among the three age groups of customers has been analysed to exhibit their level of perception on the five SQFs. The perception score on the SQFs has been computed with the help of mean of perception score on all variables included in each factor. The 'F' statistics have been computed with the help of one way analysis of variance, to reveal the significant difference among the three age groups regarding their level of perception. The results are given in Table 5.7.

Table 5.7: Customer's Perception on Service Quality (SERVPERF Scale)

Sl. No.	SQFs	Mean score among customers in			F-Statistics
		Youngsters	Middle aged	Aged	
1.	Reliability	3.4508	3.2445	3.1086	1.8508
2.	Responsiveness	3.1479	3.4556	3.0969	2.1344
3.	Assurance	3.5332	3.0965	2.6861	3.2345*
4.	Tangibles	2.7344	3.0961	3.2748	1.3365
5.	Empathy	2.7437	3.7142	3.4503	3.4508*

* Significant at five per cent level

The highly perceived SQFs among the youngsters are assurance and reliability since their mean scores are 3.5332 and 3.4508 respectively whereas among the middle aged customers these SQFs are empathy and responsiveness their respective mean scores being 3.7142 and 3.4556. Among the aged customers, the highly perceived SQFs are empathy and tangibles since their respective mean scores are 3.4503 and 3.2748. Regarding the level of perception, the significant difference among the three age groups of customers has been noticed in the perception on assurance and empathy since their respective 'F' statistics are significant at five per cent level.

SERVQUAL Scale on SQFs Among the Customers

The SERVQUAL scale in each SQF is computed by the difference between the level of perception and expectation on each SQF among the customers. The mean of SERVQUAL scale on five SQFs among the three groups of customers has been computed to exhibit the level of deviation of perception from its expectation. Regarding the SERVQUAL scale on all five SQFs, the significant difference among the three age groups of customers has been analysed with the help of one way analysis of variance. The results are given in Table 5.8.

Table 5.8: SERVQUAL Scale Among the Customers

Sl. No.	SQFs	Mean Score Among Customers			F-Statistics
		Youngsters	Middle aged	Aged	
1.	Reliability	-0.7578	-0.5742	0.03617	3.9196*
2.	Responsiveness	-0.9968	-0.2746	-0.3070	2.9969*
3.	Assurance	-0.7391	-0.5586	-1.0960	2.0344
4.	Tangibles	-1.1215	-0.2448	0.2305	3.5157*
5.	Empathy	-1.0997	-0.1544	-0.7606	3.4308*

* Significant at five per cent level.

The SERVQUAL scale on tangibles among the aged customers is 0.2305. It reveals that the aged customers are satisfied upto their level of expectation regarding the 'tangible' factor. It is followed by the 'reliability' factor among the aged customers since its mean score is 0.03617. In all other cases, the mean of SERVQUAL scale among the three age groups of customers is negative. It represents the level of expectation on the SQFs is higher than its respective perception on SQFs among the young and middle aged customers. Among the aged customers, it is seen in responsiveness, assurance and empathy since their respective SERVQUAL scales are negative. Regarding the SERVQUAL scale, the significant difference among the three age groups of customers has been identified in reliability, responsiveness, tangibles and empathy since their respective 'F' statistics are significant at five per cent level.

Customers Satisfaction Index Among Different Age Groups

The customer satisfaction is measured with the help of an index called Customers Satisfaction Index (CSI). The CSI in the present study is confined to less than 21 per cent, 21 to 40, 41 to 60, 61 to 80 and above 80 per cent. The distribution of customers on the basis of their CSI is presented in Table 5.9.

Table 5.9: Customer Satisfaction Index (CSI) Among the Different Age Groups of Customers

Sl. No.	CSI (in per cent)	Number of Customers in			Total
		Youngsters	Middle Aged	Aged	
1.	Less than 21	36	38	19	83
2.	21- 40	59	73	19	151
3.	41- 60	61	86	45	192
4.	61- 80	42	35	45	122
5.	Above 80	19	27	29	75
	Total	**217**	**259**	**147**	**623**

The important CSI among the customers is 41 to 60 and 21 to 40 per cent which constitute 30.82 and 24.23 per cent to their respective total. The customers with the CSI of less than 21 per cent constitutes 13.32 per cent of the total. The most important CSI among the young customers is 41 to 60 per cent which constitutes 28.11 per cent of its total whereas among the middle aged, it is also 41 to 60 per cent which constitutes 33.20 per cent of its total. Among the aged customers, it is 61 to 80 and 41 to 60 per cent which constitutes 30.61 per cent each of their total. The analysis infers that the aged customers are more satisfied than the middle aged and young customers.

Impact of SERVPERF Scale of SQFs on the CSI Among Different Age Groups of Customers

The relative influence of the SERVPERF scale of SQFs on the customers' level of satisfaction (CSI) is examined to reveal the importance of SQFs in the customer satisfaction among different age groups. The perception score on the five SQFs is treated as the score of independent variables whereas the CSI is considered as the score of dependent variables. The impact of independent variables on the dependent variables is examined with the help of multiple regression analysis. The results are given in Table 5.10.

Table 5.10: Impact of SERVPERF Scale of SQFS on CSI

Sl. No.	SQFs	Regression Co-efficients among Customers		
		Youngsters	Middle aged	Aged
1.	Reliability	0.1408*	0.0818	0.2417*
2.	Responsiveness	0.0921	0.1816*	0.2133*
3.	Assurance	0.1661*	0.2145*	0.0948
4.	Tangibles	0.1024	0.0776	0.1471*
5.	Empathy	0.0439	0.1337*	0.2803*
	Constant	0.8565	1.3817	1.8916
	R2	0.6962	0.7412	0.7966
	F-Statistics	8.4336*	10.2449*	12.3908*

Among the youngsters, the significantly influencing SQFs on their CSI are reliability and assurance. A unit increase in the perception on above said two SQFs would result in an increase in CSI by 0.1408 and 0.1661 units respectively. Among the middle aged customers, the significant independent variables are responsiveness, assurance and empathy since their respective regression coefficients are significant at five per cent level. A unit increase in the perception on above said three SQFs would result in an increase in CSI by 0.1816, 0.2145 and 0.1337 units respectively.

The significantly influencing SQFs on the CSI among the aged customers are reliability, responsiveness, tangibles and empathy since their respective regression coefficients are significant at five per cent level. A unit increase in the perception on the above said SQFs would result in an increase in CSI by 0.2417, 0.213, 0.1471 and 0.2803 units respectively. The changes in the perception on SQFs explain the changes in CSI to the extent of 79.66 per cent, since their respective R^2 is 0.7966.

The analysis reveals that the perception of SQFs is high and has a more positive influence on CSI among the aged customers than the middle age customers. The young customer is not easily influenced by the SQFs of the commercial banks.

Discriminate SQFs Among the Three Age Groups of Customers

Based on age, the customers are classified into youngsters, middle aged and aged. The perception on the SQFs among the three different age groups of customers may differ because the level of exposure, knowledge, expectations and comparison of the service with the other available services differ among the three groups of customers. The bank managers have to understand the level of perception on SQFs among the three age groups of customers. Only then they can provide right service to the right customers segment. For the policy implications, they have to identify the important discriminate SQFs among the three groups. The multiple discriminate analysis have been administered to identify the important discriminate SQFs among the three groups. Initially the mean score of SQFs among the three aged group of customers, its respective 'F' statistics and Wilk's Lambda coefficients have been computed and presented in Table 5.11.

Table 5.11: Mean Difference and Discriminate Power of SQFS

Sl. No.	SQFs	Mean Score among customers			F-Statistics	P-value	Wilk's Lambda
		Youngs-ters	Middle Aged	Aged			
1.	Reliability	3.4508	3.2445	3.1086	1.8508	0.2171	0.5868
2.	Responsiveness	3.1479	3.4556	3.0969	2.1344	0.1346	0.4331
3.	Assurance	3.5332	3.0965	2.6861	3.2345	0.0501	0.1817
4.	Tangibles	2.7344	3.0961	3.2748	1.3365	0.3096	0.2776
5.	Empathy	2.7437	3.7142	3.4503	3.4508	0.0348	0.1345

The highly perceived SQFs among the young customers are assurance and reliability since their respective mean scores are 3.5332 and 3.4508. Among the middle aged customers, these SQFs are empathy and responsiveness since their respective mean scores are 3.7142 and 3.4556. The highly perceived SQFs among the aged customers are empathy and tangibles since their respective mean scores are 3.4503 and 3.2748. Regarding the perception on SQFs, the significant difference among the three age groups of customers has been noticed in the case of empathy and assurance since their respective 'F' statistics are significant at five per cent level. The higher discriminate power is noticed in the case of empathy and assurances since their respective Wilk's Lambda are 0.1345 and 0.1817.

Canonical Discriminate Function

In the present analysis, the number of group are three. Hence, a maximum of only 2 functions can be generated. The first function has the highest ratio between groups to within group sum of squares. The second function uncorrelated with the first, has the second highest ratio and so on. However, not all the functions may be statically significant. The eigen value per cent of variance and canonical correlation of the two functions are summarised in Table 5.12.

Table 5.12: Canonical Discriminate Function

Function	Eigen Value	Per cent of Variance	Cumulative per cent of Variance	Canonical Correlation	After Function	Wilk' Lambda	Chi-Square Value	P-Value
1.	5.0345	89.01	89.01	0.7339	0	0.1862	39.4146	0.0000
2.	0.6861	10.09	100.00	0.2841	1	0.7391	2.0941	0.4146

The eigen value associated with the first function is 5.0345 and this accounts for 89.01 per cent of the explained variance. Because of the high eigen value, the first function is declared as superior. The second function has a small eigen value of 0.6861 and accounts for only 10.09 per cent of the explained variance. The '0' below after function indicates that no function has been removed. The value of Wilk's Lambda is 0.1862. This transforms to a chi-square of 39.4146, which is significant at zero per cent level. Thus the two functions, together, significantly discriminate the three age groups of customers. However, the Wilk's Lambda of the second function is 0.7391, which is not significant at five per cent level. Therefore, the second function is declared to be not contributing significantly on the group differences.

Discriminate Coefficient of the Various SQFs

The discriminate coefficient of the SQFs in the first and second functions has been computed with the help of standardized discriminate function. The study has already proved the non validity of the second function. Anyhow, the discriminate coefficients of the five SQFs in function-1 and function-2 are summarized in Table 5.13.

Table 5.13: Standardised Canonical Discriminate Function Coefficients

Sl. No.	SQFs	Functions	
		Function-1	Function-2
1.	Reliability	0.1334	0.3348
2.	Responsiveness	0.2641	-0.2969
3.	Assurance	0.4541	0.1403
4.	Tangibles	1.3084	-0.1809
5.	Empathy	1.8182	0.2141
	Per cent of cases correctly classified	81.29	49.34

Only the first function has been included for the interpretation purpose. According to function-1, the important discriminate SQFs among the three different groups of customers are empathy, tangibles and assurance since their respective discriminate coefficients are 1.8182, 1.3084 and 0.4541. The analysis reveals that the three different age groups of customers are discriminated on the basis of their perception on empathy, tangibles and assurance. It is highly useful for the bank managers to design their service strategy in such way as to satisfy all groups of customers according to their needs and perceptions.

Gender wise Segmentation Analysis

Gender segmentation has grown in use over the years as marketers have recognized that women are a lucrative market segment; and therefore marketers have become more sensitive to women's attitudes and needs (Kotler and Armstrong, 1991)[4]. More recently, evidence revealing the women's involvement in financial decisions in the household has been uncovered (Plank et al., 1994)[5]. Hence, understanding the key differences between males and females regarding their level of expectation and perception on service quality factors is becoming critical. Previous researchers (Thompson and Kaminski, 1993[6]; Welster, 1989[7]; and Gagliano and Sivey, 1993) found the significant relationship between the gender and the level of expectation and perception on SQFs.

Gender Wise Customers' Perception on SQFs

The perception on SQFs among the male and female customers has been measured with the help of mean score of the perception on the SQFs namely reliability, responsiveness, assurance, tangibles and empathy. The scores of the above said five SQFs have been computed by the mean score of the variables in each factor. The significant difference among the male and female customers has been examined with the help of 't' test. The resultant mean score of perception on SQFs and their respective 't' statistics are shown in Table 5.14.

Table 5.14: Gender Wise Customer Perception on Service Quality (SERVPERF Scale)

Sl. No.	SQFs	Mean Score Among Customers		'T'-Statistics
		Male	Female	
1.	Reliability	3.1443	3.7856	-2.2144*
2.	Responsiveness	3.0217	4.1307	-2.8969*
3.	Assurance	3.0589	3.4845	-1.5317
4.	Tangibles	2.8997	3.4155	-1.9903*
5.	Empathy	3.2021	3.7142	-1.6568

* Significant at five per cent level.

The highly perceived SQFs among the male customers are empathy and reliability since their respective mean scores are 3.2021 and 3.1443. Among the female customers these

SQFs are responsiveness and reliability since their respective mean scores are 4.1307 and 3.7856. In total, the female customers have higher perception on all SQFs than the male customers. But, the significant difference among the male and female customers has been identified in the perception on reliability, responsiveness and tangibles since their respective 't' statistics are significant at five per cent level.

SERVQUAL Scale on SQFs

The difference between the perception and expectation on the five SQFs among the male and female customers has been analysed to exhibit the level of difference between their perception and expectation on each SQF. It is highly essential to identify the gap for policy implication related to the reduction of gap between perception and expectation. Regarding the SERVQUAL scale, the significant difference among the male and female customers has been analysed with the help of 't' test. The results are given in Table 5.15.

Table 5.15: SERVQUAL Scale Among Male and Female Customers

Sl. No.	SQFs	Mean Score among customers		'T'-statistics
		Male	Female	
1.	Reliability	-0.4441	-0.6727	-2.0011*
2.	Responsiveness	-0.6345	-0.1732	2.0456*
3.	Assurance	-0.8292	-0.4590	1.9801*
4.	Tangibles	0.4042	-0.5591	-0.9104
5.	Empathy	-0.6121	-0.7202	-0.8543

* Significant at five per cent level.

In all five SQFs, the SERVQUAL scale is negative. It represents that the customers are not satisfied to their level of expectation. The higher SERVQUAL scale among the male customers is noticed in the case of assurance and responsiveness since their mean scores are -0.8292 and -0.6345 respectively. Among the female customers, these SQFs are empathy and reliability since their respective mean scores are -0.7202 and -0.6727. The SERVQUAL scale on assurance and responsiveness among the male customers is greater than the female customers. Regarding the SERVQUAL scale, the significant difference among the male and female customers have been noticed in the case of reliability, responsiveness and assurance since their respective 't' statistics are significant at five per cent level.

Customer Satisfaction Index (CSI) Among the Male and Female Customers

The levels of satisfaction among the customers have been derived by the scores on the related statements. It is summated with the help of an index called Customer Satisfaction Index (CSI). The CSI reveals the overall picture of the level of customer satisfaction towards the banks among the male and female customers. In the present study, the CSI is confined to less than 21 per cent, 21 to 40, 41 to 60, 61 to 80 and above 80 per cent. The distribution of customers on the basis of their CSI is given in Table 5.16.

Table 5.16: Customer Satisfaction Index (CSI) Among Male and Female Customers

Sl. No.	CSI (in per cent)	Number of Customers in		Total
		Male	Female	
1.	Less than 21	39	19	58
2.	21-40	148	28	176
3.	41-60	187	55	242
4.	61-80	89	17	106
5.	Above 80	24	17	41
	Total	**487**	**136**	**623**

The important CSIs among the customers are 41 to 60 per cent and 21 to 40 per cent which constitute 38.84 and 28.25 per cent to their respective total. The customers with an index of above 80 per cent contributes 6.58 per cent of the total. The important CSI among the male customers are 41 to 60 and 21 to 40 per cent which constitute 38.39 and 30.39 per cent their respective total. Among the female customers, the two important CSI also 41 to 60 and 21 to 40 per cent but these two constitutes 40.44 and 20.59 per cent to their respective total. Regarding the customer satisfaction, there is no major difference between the male and female customers.

Impact of SERVPERF Scale of SQFs on Customers Satisfaction

The importance of the perception on SQFs, in explaining the changes in customer satisfaction has been examined, with the help of multiple regression analysis. The included independent variables are the perception on SQFs whereas the dependent variable is their CSI. The impact of perception on SQFs on the CSI among the male and female customers has been examined separately. The resulting regression coefficients of SQFs is summarized in Table 5.17.

Table 5.17: Impact of SERVPERF Scale of SQFS on CSI

Sl. No.	SQFs	Regression coefficients among customers	
		Male	Female
1.	Reliability	0.2217*	0.1044
2.	Responsiveness	0.1414*	0.2104*
3.	Assurance	0.0962	0.1616*
4.	Tangibles	0.1084	0.2069*
5.	Empathy	0.0869	0.3144*
	Constant	0.9946	1.2142
	R^2	0.8241	0.7433
	F-Statistics	14.9817*	10.3914*

* Significant at five per cent level.

The significantly influencing SQFs on the CSI among the male customers are reliability and responsiveness since their regression coefficients are significant at five per cent level. A unit increase in the perception on reliability and responsiveness would result in an increase in CSI by 0.2217 and 0.1414 units respectively. Among the female customers, the significantly influencing SQFs on the CSI are responsiveness, assurance, tangibles and empathy. A unit increase in the perception on the above said SQFs results in an increase in their CSI by 0.2104, 0.1616, 0.2069 and 0.3144 units respectively. The changes in the perception on SQFs explain the changes in their CSI among the female customers to the extent of 74.33 per cent. The analysis reveals that the perceptions on SQFs have a higher influence on CSI among the female customers than among the male customers. The important SQFs among the female customers are empathy and responsiveness whereas among the male customers, it is reliability.

Discriminate SQFs Among the Male and Female Customers

The male and female customers' perception on SQFs are different because of their level of expectation, knowledge and awareness on the banking activities and also the competitive services offered by the other banks. Usually, the male customers have more awareness on all aspects related to banking than their counterparts, while the female customers expect more from the bankers than the male customers. It is highly imperative to identify the important discriminate SQFs among the male and female customers. The two group discriminate analysis has been followed, to identify the important discriminate SQFs. Initially, the mean difference among male and female customers especially on all the five SQFs and their respective 't' statistics and the discriminate power of the SQFs have been computed. The results are given in Table 5.18.

Table 5.18: Mean Difference and Discriminate Power of SQFS

Sl. No.	SQFs	Mean score among customers		Mean difference	'T' Statistics	Wilk's Lambda
		Male	Female			
1.	Reliability	3.1443	3.7856	-0.6413	-2.8473*	0.2696
2.	Responsiveness	3.0217	4.1307	-1.1090	-4.1449*	0.1081
3.	Assurance	3.0589	3.4845	-0.4256	-1.8081	0.5197
4.	Tangibles	2.8997	3.4155	-0.5158	-2.6081*	0.2456
5.	Empathy	3.2021	3.7142	-0.5121	-2.4132*	0.1432

* Significant at five per cent level.

The higher perception on SQFs among the male customers is noticed in empathy and reliability since their respective mean scores are 3.2021 and 3.1443. Among the female customers, the SQFs with high perception are responsiveness and reliability since their respective mean scores are 4.1307 and 3.7856. The higher mean difference is noticed in the case of responsiveness and reliability since their respective mean differences are -1.1090 and -0.6413. The significant mean difference is identified in the case of reliability, responsiveness, tangibles and empathy since their respective 't' statistics are significant at five per cent level. The higher mean difference is noticed in the case of responsiveness and empathy since the respective Wilk's Lambda are 0.1081 and 0.1432.

The significant SQFs have been included to establish the two group discriminate function. The unstandardised procedure has been followed to establish the function. The estimated function is:

$$Z = 0.8982 - 0.2144X_1 - 0.2968X_2 - 0.1863X_4 - 0.3141X_5$$

The relative contribution of SQFs in total discriminate score, is computed by the product of the discriminate coefficient and the respective mean difference of the SQFs. The results are given in Table 5.19.

Table 5.19: Relative Contribution of SQFS in Total Discriminate Score (TDS)

Sl. No.	SQFs	Canonical Discriminate Coefficient	Mean Difference	Product	Relative Contribution in TDS (in per cent)
1.	Reliability	-0.2144	-0.6413	0.1375	18.99
2.	Responsiveness	-0.2968	-1.1090	0.3292	45.49
3.	Tabgibles	-0.1863	-0.5158	0.0961	13.29
4.	Empathy	-0.3141	-0.5121	0.1609	22.23
	Total			**0.7237**	**100.00**
	Per cent of cases correctly classified: 71.86				

The higher discriminate coefficient is noticed in empathy and responsiveness since their discriminate coefficients are -0.3141 and -0.2968 respectively. It reveals that the above said two SQFs have more influence on the discriminate function. The higher relative contribution in TDS is identified in responsiveness and empathy since their relative contributions are 45.49 and 22.23 per cent to their respective total. The established discriminate function correctly classifies the cases to the extent of 71.86 per cent. The analysis reveals that the important discriminate SQFs among the male and female customers are responsiveness and empathy whereas the female customers show more perception than the male customers.

Customer Segmentation Analysis Based on Education

The level of education among the customers is one of the important profiles of the customers in the banking industry. The educated customers may be aware of the available banking services, the banking environments and its latest development. Hence the educated customers may expect more competitive and innovative services from their bankers. The less educated customers are always expecting core services from their bankers. It is highly important to analyse the expectation and perception on the service quality of commercial banks among the less educated and highly educated customers in order to identify the basic differences among them.

In the presently study, the levels of education among the customers is confined to less educated, educated and highly educated. The less educated customer group consists of the customers with the educational qualification of less than 10th standard and 10th standard. The educated customers are customers with the educational qualification of higher secondary level and under-graduation level. The customers with post graduation and professional education are included in the highly educated customer group. In total, out of 623 customers, 136 customers are less educated whereas 307 customers are educated. The highly educated customers are 180 in number.

Perception on SQFs among Different Educated Groups of Customers

The level of perception on SQFs among the three different educated groups of customers has been analysed to show their level of perception on SQFs. The perception scores on SQFs have been computed by the mean score of perception on all variables in each factor. The one way analysis of variance has been executed to analyse the significant difference among the three groups of customers regarding their level of perception. The results are given in Table 5.20. (*See Table on next page*)

The highly perceived SQFs among the less educated customers are responsiveness and reliability since their mean scores are 3.0144 and 2.9697 respectively. Among the educated customers, these SQFs are empathy and responsiveness since their respective mean scores are 3.2021 and 3.1334. The highly perceived SQFs among the highly educated customers are reliability and empathy since their respective mean scores are 3.9100 and 3.8024. Regarding the perception on SQFs, the significant difference among the three groups of educated customers has been identified in the perception on reliability and empathy since their respective 'F' statistics are significant at five per cent level.

Table 5.20: Perception on SQFS (SERVPERF Scale) Among Different Educated Groups Customers

Sl. No.	SQFs	Mean Score among customers			F-Statistics
		Less Educated	Educated	Highly Educated	
1.	Reliability	2.9697	3.0568	3.9100	2.9997*
2.	Responsiveness	3.0144	3.1334	3.6747	1.8904
3.	Assurance	2.8441	3.0216	3.6063	1.4536
4.	Tangibles	2.6239	2.9334	3.4403	2.0147
5.	Empathy	2.9196	3.2021	3.8024	2.9909*

* Significant at five per cent level.

SERVQUAL Scale Among the Different Educated Groups

The SERVQUAL scale indicates the difference between the level of perception and expectation on the SQFs of commercial banks. The negative SERVQUAL scale reveals that the level of perception on SQFs is less than its level of expectation. The mean of SERVQUAL scale on SQFs among the less educated, educated and highly educated customers have been computed separately. The one way analysis of variance has been executed to analyse the significant difference among the three groups. (*See Table on next page*)

Table 5.21 explains the mean of SERVQUAL scale on SQFs among the three groups of customers and their respective 'F' statistics. In all cases, the SERVQUAL scale is identified as negative. It reveals that the level of perception on SQFs is not upto the expectation of customers. The higher negative SERVQUAL scale among the less educated customers has been identified in empathy and assurance since their respective mean scores are -1.2973 and -0.8732. Among the educated customers, these two variables are assurance and responsiveness since their respective mean scores are -0.8466 and -0.7183 whereas among the highly educated customers, these are identified in reliability and assurance since their mean scores are -0.5057 and -0.4866 respectively. Regarding the SERVQUAL scale, the significant difference among the three groups of customers has been identified in the case of reliability, responsiveness, tangibles and empathy since their respective 'F' statistics are significant at five per cent level.

Table 5.21: SERVQUAL Scale Among the Different Educated Customers

Sl. No.	SQFs	Mean score among customers			F-Statistics
		Less Educated	Educated	Highly Educated	
1.	Reliability	-0.1730	-0.6293	-0.5057	2.9913*
2.	Responsiveness	-0.2742	-0.7183	-0.4151	3.1415*
3.	Assurance	-0.8732	-0.8466	-0.4866	2.5862
4.	Tangibles	-0.4217	-0.6283	-0.1258	3.2026*
5.	Empathy	-1.2973	-0.7113	-0.0007	4.1718*

* Significant at five per cent level.

Customer Satisfaction Index Among Different Educated Groups of Customers

The customer satisfaction among the customers has been measured with the help of some related statements. The customers' view on these statements are summated with the help of an index called Customer Satisfaction Index (CSI). The CSI in the present study is confined to less than 21 per cent, 21 to 40, 41 to 60, 61 to 80 and above 80 per cent. The distribution of customers on the basis of their CSI is illustrated in Table 5.22.

Table 5.22: Customer Satisfaction Index (CSI) Among Different Educated Customers

Sl. No.	CSI (in per cent)	Number of Customers			Total
		Lesser Educated	Educated	Highly Educated	
1.	Less than 21	10	26	21	57
2.	21-40	22	27	60	109
3.	41-60	39	169	41	249
4.	61-80	38	48	39	125
5.	Above 80	27	37	19	83
	Total	**136**	**307**	**180**	**623**

The important CSI among the customers are 41 to 60 and 61 to 80 per cent which constitute 39.97 and 20.06 per cent of the total. The important CSI among the less educated customers are 41 to 60 and 61 to 80 per cent which constitute 28.68 and 27.94 per cent to their respective total. Among the educated customers, the important CSI is 41 to 60 per cent which constitutes 55.05 per cent of its total. Among the highly educated customers, these are 21 to 40 per cent and 41 to 60 per cent which constitute 33.33 and 22.78 per cent to their respective total. Higher level of satisfaction is identified among the less educated customers whereas low level of satisfaction is identified among the highly educated customers.

Impact of SQFs on CSI Among Different Education Groups

The perception on SQFs among the three groups of customers based on education may have its own impact on the CSI. It is imperative to identify the significantly influencing SQFs on CSI and also compare the degree of influence of each SQF on the CSI among each group of customers separately for some policy implications. The multiple regression analysis has been executed to analyse such impact. The resultant regression coefficients are given in Table 5.23.

Table 5.23: Impact of SERVPERF Scale of SQFS on CSI

Sl. No.	SQFs	Regression Co-efficients among Customers		
		Less Educated	Educated	Highly Educated
1.	Reliability	0.1013	0.2117*	0.2021*
2.	Responsiveness	0.2817*	0.1338*	0.1917*
3.	Assurance	0.1868*	0.1142	0.1436*
4.	Tangibles	0.0866	0.0911	0.1011
5.	Empathy	0.1217	0.1904*	0.1803*
	Constant	0.8587	1.2348	1.4508
	R2	0.6247	0.7667	0.8134
	F-Statistics	7.5868*	10.3441*	12.4561*

* Significant at five per cent level.

The significantly influencing SQFs on CSI among the less educated customers are responsiveness and assurance since their respective regression co-efficient are significant at five per cent level. A unit increase in the perception on responsiveness and assurance would result in an increase in CSI by 0.2817 and 0.1868 units respectively. Among the educated customers, these significant SQFs are reliability, responsiveness and empathy. A unit increase in the perception on the above said three SQFs would result in an increase in CSI by 0.2117, 0.1338 and 0.1904 units respectively.

Among the highly educated customers, the significantly influencing SQFs are reliability, responsiveness, assurance and empathy. A unit increase in the perception on the above said SQFs, would result in an increase in CSI by 0.2021, 0.1917, 0.1436 and 0.1803 units respectively. The changes in the perception on SQFs explain the changes in the CSI among the higher educated customers which are identified as higher to the extent of 81.34 per cent. The analysis reveals that the perceptions on SQFs have higher impact on CSI among the highly educated customers than the other two groups of customers.

Discriminate SQFs Among the Different Educated Groups of Customers

The higher educated customers' level of perception and expectations are usually higher than the less educated customers since their level of exposure, knowledge, expectations and other things are higher. At the same time, the less educated customers may expect more from their banks because they lack in knowledge and exposure of the present banking environment. The service provider should know the level of expectation and perception on the SQFs in commercial banks among different groups of customers with different levels of education. Then only they can give the right service to the right customers. Apart from this, they have to know the important discriminate SQFs among the three groups of customers for some policy implications. Hence, the present analysis has made an attempt on this aspect. Initially, the mean of the perception on SQFs, its statistical significance and the discriminate power of the SQFs have been computed and presented in Table 5.24.

Table 5.24: Mean Difference and Discriminate Power of SQFS

Sl. No.	SQFs	Mean Score among Customers			F-Statistics	P-value	Wilk's Lambda
		Lesser Educated	Educated	Highly Educated			
1.	Reliability	2.9697	3.0568	3.9100	2.9997	0.0144	0.1338
2.	Responsiveness	3.0144	3.1334	3.6747	1.8904	0.1656	0.2846
3.	Assurance	2.8441	3.0216	3.6063	1.4536	0.2131	0.4816
4.	Tangibles	2.6239	2.9334	3.4403	2.0147	0.0868	0.3992
5.	Empathy	2.9196	3.2021	3.8024	2.9909	0.0217	0.1081

The highly educated customers perceive more on the SQFs than the other two groups of customers. The significant difference among the three groups of customers has been identified in the perception on reliability and empathy since their respective 'F' statistics are significant at five per cent level. The higher discriminate power of the SQFs is identified in the case of empathy and reliability since their Wilk's Lambda are 0.1081 and 0.1338 respectively.

Canonical Discriminate Function

The number of groups included in the present analysis is three. Hence the present study can generate a maximum of two discriminate functions. The validity and reliability of the functions are examined with the help of its eigen value, per cent of variance, Wilk's Lambda and the level of significance of the chi-square value. Out of the functions generated by the discriminate analysis, only one function is selected for the interpretation purposes. The validity and reliability of the two functions generated by the multi discriminate analysis are given in Table 5.25.

Table 5.25: Canonical Discriminate Functions

Function	Eigen Value	Per cent of Variance	Cumulative per cent of	Canonical Correlation Variance	After Function	Wilk's Lambda	Chi-Square Value	P-Value
1.	3.8144	91.03	91.07	0.7984	0	0.1563	46.0334	0.0000
2.	0.2861	8.97	100.00	0.2446	1	0.8109	2.4317	0.5138

The eigen value associated with the first function is 3.8144 and this accounts for 91.03 per cent of the explained variance. Because of the high eigen value, the first function is declared as superior to the second function. The second function has a smaller eigen value of 0.2861 and accounts for only 8.97 per cent of the explained variance. The '0' below after function indicates that no function has been removed. The value of Wilk's Lambda is 0.1563. This transforms to a chi-square of 46.0334 which is significant at zero per cent level. Thus two functions together significantly, discriminate the three different educated groups of customer. However, the Wilk's Lambda of the second function is 0.8109, which is not significant at five per cent level. Therefore, the second function is declared to be not contributing significantly on group differences.

Discriminate Co-efficient of the Various SQFs

The standardized procedure has been followed to estimate the discriminate coefficients of SQFs. The analysis has established two functions namely function-1 and function-2. The function-1 above has been included for the interpretation since its reliability and validity are higher. The results of the multi discriminate analysis are shown in Table 5.26.

Table 5.26: Standardised Canonical Discriminate Function Coefficients

Sl. No.	SQFs	Function	
		Function-1	Function-2
1.	Reliability	0.8894	0.2143
2.	Responsiveness	-0.1017	0.4661
3.	Assurance	0.2786	0.2009
4.	Tangibles	0.4146	0.1886
5.	Empathy	1.2331	0.2149
	Per cent of cases correctly classified	81.08	21.96

According to the function, the established discriminate function correctly classified the cases to the extent of 81.08 per cent. The important discriminate SQFs among the three educated groups of customers are empathy and reliability since their discriminate coefficients are 1.2331 and 0.8894 respectively. The result indicates that the important discriminate SQFs among the three educated groups of customers are empathy and reliability. Hence, the service providers concentrate more on the above said two SQFs before they provide their service to the different customer segments based on their level of education.

Income Segmentation Analysis

The various income levels among the customers, may play their own role in the expectation and perception on SQFs. The higher income groups may be aware of the banking environment compared to others since the amount of their transactions and years of their experience in banking industry are high. At the same time, the lower income groups may expect according to their level of expectations from banks. The level of expectation from the different income groups may not be unique. Hence, it is highly imperative to follow differentiated marketing strategy to satisfy all income groups of customers. The bank managers have to identify the level of expectation and perception on SQFs among different income classes and also the discriminate SQFs among them, on the basis of their expectation and perception for policy implications. Hence the present analysis focuses on this aspect.

The income levels of the customers are classified into Low Income Groups (LIGs), Middle Income Groups (MIGs) and Higher Income Groups (HIGs). The Low Income Groups consists of the customers with the monthly income of less than Rs.10000 whereas the middle income groups consists of customers with the monthly income of Rs.15001 to 25000. The customers with the monthly income of above Rs.25,000 belong to Higher Income Groups.

Customers' Perception on SQFs

The customers' perception on SQFs has been estimated by the mean score of the level of perception on SQFs, among the three income groups of customers. The score on the perception on SQFs is derived from the mean score of the variables in each factor. The one way analysis of variance has been administered to find out the significant difference among the three income groups of customers regarding their perception on SQFs. The results are given in Table 5.27.

Table 5.27: Perception on SQFS (SERVPER Scale) Among Different Income Groups

Sl. No.	SQFs	Mean score among			F-Statistics
		LIG	MIG	HIG	
1.	Reliability	2.9196	3.1841	3.5858	2.9963*
2.	Responsiveness	2.8007	2.9617	3.7667	3.0144*
3.	Assurance	2.6119	3.0469	3.5683	3.1447*
4.	Tangibles	3.1144	3.2644	2.7741	2.0446
5.	Empathy	3.0996	2.8546	3.7659	3.2042*

* Significant at five per cent level.

The highly perceived SQFs among the LIG are tangibles and empathy since their respective mean scores are 3.1144 and 3.0996 whereas among the MIG, these are tangibles and reliability with their mean scores 3.2644 and 3.1841 respectively. The highly perceived SQFs among the HIGs are responsiveness and empathy since their respective mean scores are 3.7667 and 3.7659. Regarding the perception on SQFs, the significant differences among the three income groups of customers are identified in the perception on reliability, responsiveness, assurance and empathy since the respective 'F' statistics are significant at five per cent level.

SERVQUAL scale on SQFs Among Different Income Group of Customers

The SERVQUAL scale on SQFs indicates the level of deviation of perception on SQFs from their respective expectations. The SERVQUAL scale is highly essential to reduce the gap between the customers' perception and expectation on SQFs. The negative SERVQUAL scale indicates less perception on SQFs than its expected level. The is an alarming area for the bank marketers. In the present study, the SERVQUAL scale on all five SQFs among LIG, MIG and HIG has been computed. Regarding the SERVQUAL scale, the significant differences among the three groups have been examined with the help of one way analysis of variance.

Table 5.28: SERVQUAL Scale Among Different Income Groups

Sl. No.	SQFs	Mean score among			F-Statistics
		LIG	MIG	HIG	
1.	Reliability	-0.4722	-0.4228	-0.5558	0.4146
2.	Responsiveness	-0.6595	-0.7464	-0.3076	1.5069
3.	Assurance	-0.8995	-0.7973	-0.6184	0.8189
4.	Tangibles	-0.1265	-0.0667	-0.8917	3.1499*
5.	Empathy	-0.8328	-0.8492	-0.3609	2.9969*

* Significant at five per cent level.

Table 5.28 exhibits the different mean scores of SERQUAL scale on SQFs among the three groups of customers. All SERQUAL scale on SQFs is identified as negative. It infers that the level of perception on SQFs among the customers is not upto their level of expectation. The higher SERQUAL scale among the LIG is identified in assurance and empathy since their mean scores are -0.8995 and -0.8328 respectively whereas among the MIG, they are identified in empathy and assurance since their mean scores are -0.8492 and -0.7973 respectively. Among the HIG, they are identified in the case of tangibles and assurance since their respective mean scores are -0.8917 and -0.6184 respectively. Regarding the SERQUAL scale, the significant difference among the three income groups of customers has been noticed in the case of tangibles and empathy since their 'F' statistics are significant at five per cent level.

Customer Satisfaction Index (CSI) Among Different Income Groups

The customer satisfaction towards banking has been measured with the help of the customers' attitude towards various aspects related to banking. The customers' attitude towards banking is summated with the help of an index called a Customer Satisfaction Index (CSI). In the present study, the CSI among customers is confined to less than 21per cent, 21 to 40, 41 to 60, 61 to 80 and above 80 per cent. The distribution of customers on the basis of their CSI is shown in Table 5.29.

Table 5.29: Customer Satisfaction Index (CSI) Among the Customers

Sl. No.	CSI (in per cent)	Number of Customers in			Total
		LIG	MIG	HIG	
1.	Less than 21	29	26	17	72
2.	21-40	41	43	62	146
3.	41-60	66	72	123	261
4.	61-80	24	25	45	94
5.	Above 80	11	18	21	50
	Total	**171**	**184**	**268**	**623**

The important CSI among the customers are 41 to 60 and 21 to 40 per cent which constitute 41.89 and 23.43 per cent to their respective total. The number of customers with the CSI of above 80 per cent constitutes 8.03 of the total. The important CSI among the LIG are 41 to 60 and 21 to 40 per cent which constitute 38.59 and 23.98 per cent to their respective total. Among the middle Income Group, these are also 41 to 60 and 21 to 40 per cent but these constitute 39.13 and 23.37 per cent to their respective total. Among the HIG, the important CSI are 41 to 60 and 21 to 40 per cent which constitute 45.89 and 23.13 to their respective total.

Impact of SERVPERF Scale on SQFs on CSI

The perception on SQFs among the customers may have its own impact on CSI among them. The impact of SERVPERF scale of SQFs on CSI among the customer, has been examined with the help of multiple regression analysis. The impact has been examined among LIG, MIG and HIG separately. The results are given in Table 5.30.

Table 5.30: Impact of SERVPERF Scale of SQF on CSI

Sl. No.	SQFs	Regression Co-efficients among Customers in		
		LIG	MIG	HIG
1.	Reliability	0.1817*	0.2144*	0.3142*
2.	Responsiveness	0.1202	0.2639*	0.2108*
3.	Assurance	0.1144	0.0664	0.1440*
4.	Tangibles	0.0981	0.0917	0.1664*
5.	Empathy	0.2114*	0.1438*	0.1649*
	Constant	0.9411	1.2433	1.8246
	R2	0.7028	0.7949	0.8144
	F-Statistics	8.1443*	10.3842*	14.2841*

Among the LIG, the significantly influencing SQFs on CSI are reliability and empathy. A unit increase in the perceptions on the above said SQFs results in an increase in CSI among the LIG by 0.1817 and 0.2114 units respectively. The significantly influencing SERVQUAL scale on SQFs among the middle aged customers are reliability, responsiveness and empathy. A unit increase in the perception on the above said three SQFs results in an increase in CSI by 0.2144, 0.2639 and 0.1438 units respectively.

Among the HIG, the significantly influencing SQFs on the CSI are reliability, responsiveness, assurance, tangibles and empathy. A unit increase in the perception on the above said SQFs results in an increase in CSI by 0.3142, 0.2108, 0.1440, and 0.1649 respectively. The changes in the perception on SQFs, explain the changes in CSI among the HIG to the extent of 81.44 per cent. The analysis reveals that the perception on SQFs is relatively influencing on the CSI at a higher rate among the HIG than among the MIG and LIG customers.

Discriminate SQFs Among the Three Income Groups

Since the levels of perception on SQFs among the three income groups are different, the present study has made an attempt on identifying the important discriminate SQFs, among the three income groups of customers, for some policy implications. Initially, the mean score of perception on five SQFs, its 'F' statistics, its 'P' value and the discriminate power of the SQFs have been computed and presented in Table 5.31.

Table 5.31: Mean Difference and Discriminate Power of SQFS

Sl. No.	SQFs	Mean Score among Customers			F-Statistics	P-Value	Wilk's Lambda
		LIG	MIG	HIG			
1.	Reliability	2.9196	3.1841	3.5858	2.9963	0.0514	0.1733
2.	Responsiveness	2.8007	2.9617	3.7667	3.0144	0.0411	0.2144
3.	Assurance	2.6119	3.0469	3.5683	3.1447	0.0349	0.2041
4.	Tangibles	3.1144	3.2644	2.7744	2.7741	0.0916	0.4561
5.	Empathy	3.0996	2.8546	3.7659	3.2042	0.0124	0.1021

The significant mean difference in the perception on SQFs among the three income groups of customers has been identified in the case of reliability, responsiveness, assurance and empathy since their respective 'F' statistics are significant at five per cent level. The lower Wilk's Lambda has been noticed in the case of empathy and reliability since their respective Wilk's Lambda are 0.1021 and 0.1733. It reveals that the discriminate power of the above two SQFs is higher in discriminating the three income groups of customers.

Canonical Discriminate Function

The income groups among the customers have been classified into LIG, MIG and HIG. The multi-discriminate analysis can generate to a maximum of two discriminate functions since the number of groups minus one is equal to two. The first function has the highest ratio between the groups to the group sum of squares. The second function uncorrelated with the first, has the second highest ratio and so on. However, not all the functions may be statistically significant. The eigen value, per cent of variance and canonical correlation of the functions are summarised in Table 5.32.

Table 5.32: Canonical Discriminate Function

Function	Eigen value	Per cent of variance	Cumulative per cent of variance	Canonical correlation	After function	Wilk's Lambda	Chi-Square value	P-Value
1.	4.1039	91.82	91.82	0.8104	0	0.1433	46.0496	0.0000
2.	0.5191	8.18	100.00	0.1497	1	0.8192	3.1408	0.5142

The eigen value associated with the first function is 4.1039 and this accounts for 91.82 per cent of the explained variance. Because of the high eigen value, the first function is declared as superior over the other functions. The second function has a smaller eigen value of 0.5191 and accounts for only 8.18 per cent of the explained variance. The '0' below after function indicates that no function has been removed. The value of Wilk's Lambda is 0.1433. This transforms to a chi-square of 46.0496, which is significant at zero per cent level. Thus the two functions together significantly discriminate the three income groups. However, the Wilk's Lambda of the second function is 0.8192 which is not significant at five per cent level. Therefore, the second function is declared to be not contributing significantly to the group differences.

Discriminate Coefficients of the Various SQFs

The discriminate coefficients of the SQFs have been derived from the established discriminate function, based on standardized method. Since the analysis has proved the non-validity of the second function, the first function above has been included for further interpretation. The results are summarized in Table 5.33.

Table 5.33: Standardised Canonical Discriminate Function Coefficients

Sl. No.	SQFs	Functions	
		Function-1	Function-2
1.	Reliability	0.4546	0.2102
2.	Responsiveness	0.1688	0.0444
3.	Assurance	0.2133	-0.1786
4.	Tangibles	-0.1788	0.4344
5.	Empathy	0.5451	0.1058
	Per cent of cases correctly classified	81.56	21.44

According to the function-1, the important discriminate service quality factors among the three income groups of customers are empathy and reliability since their respective discriminate coefficients are 0.5451 and 0.4546. The analysis infers the importance of empathy and reliability factors to frame the differentiated marketing strategy to a different income group of customers.

Service Quality in Different Benefit Seekers

Based on benefit factor, the customers are classified into two important groups namely convenience seekers and performance seekers. The convenience seekers are the customers who are giving more on the accessibility, ATM facilities, Teller system, convenience location and hours to select the present bank for their bank transactions. The performance seekers are the customers who are expecting more financial and non-financial benefits from the banks. They are always comparing the services offered by the banks and also the cost of service charged by the banks. These customers are usually selecting a particular branch as their bank just for the purpose of the performance of the bank which meets their expectations. These two benefit segmentations are technically different from each other. The level of expectation and perception on the service quality factors among the two types of customers differ significantly. Hence, it is imperative for the bank manager to understand the nature of customers and their level of expectation and perception on SQFs for future policy implications. The present study has made an attempt to analyse this aspect in detail.

Perception on SQFs among Convenience and Performance Seekers

The level of perception on SQFs among the two types of customers may differ from each other. In order to analyse these aspects, the levels of perception on SQFs among the two groups of customers, have been computed separately. The perception scores on SQFs have been derived from the mean score of perception on the service quality variables in each factor. The analysis of the significant difference among the two types of customers, regarding their level of perception on SQF is made with the help of 't' test. The results are given in Table 5.34. (*See Table on next page*)

The highly perceived SQFs among the convenience seekers are empathy and tangibles since their respective mean scores are 3.2021 and 3.1481. Among the performance seekers, the highly perceived SQFs are empathy and responsiveness since their respective mean scores are 3.8490 and 3.4367. Regarding the perception on the SQFs, the significant differences among the convenience and performance seekers have been identified in the perception of the service qualities namely reliability, responsiveness, assurance and empathy since their respective 't' statistics are significant at five per cent level.

Table 5.34: Perception on SQFS (SERVPER Scale) Among Convenience and Performance Seekers

Sl. No.	SQFs	Mean Score among Customers		'T'-statistics
		CSR	PSR	
1.	Reliability	2.9194	3.3990	-1.9854*
2.	Responsiveness	2.7138	3.4367	-2.6339*
3.	Assurance	2.5066	3.3546	-28411*
4.	Tangibles	3.1481	2.9698	0.5768
5.	Empathy	3.2021	3.8490	-2.1819*

* Significant at five per cent level.

SERVQUAL scale on SQFs Among the Convenience and Performance Seekers

The difference between the perception and expectation on the service quality of the commercial banks is called as the SERVQUAL scale on SQFs. The SERVQUAL scale on SQFs has been examined to reduce the gap between the perception and expectation on the SQFs among the two groups of customers. The negative SERVQUAL scale indicates that the level of perception on SQFs is less than the respective level of expectation on the SQFs. The 't' test has been administered to find out the significant difference among the convenience and performance seekers regarding their SERVQUAL scale on SQFs. (*See Table on next page*)

Table 5.35 explains the mean of SERVQUAL scale on SQFs among the convenience and performance seekers and their respective 't' statistics. The higher SERVQUAL scale among the convenience seekers is identified in empathy and assurance since their respective mean scores are -1.0144 and

-0.9439 whereas among the performance seekers, it is identified in the case of assurance and responsiveness since their respective mean scores are -0.6866 and -0.5757. Regarding the SERVQUAL scale on the SQFs, the significant difference among the two types of customers has been identified in the case of assurance and empathy since their respective 't' statistics are significant at five per cent level.

Table 5.35: SERVQUAL Scale Among the Convenience and Performance Seekers

Sl. No.	SQFs	Mean Score among Customers		'T'-Statistics
		CSR	PSR	
1.	Reliability	-0.4452	-.5093	-0.9169
2.	Responsiveness	-0.4004	-0.5757	-1.2842
3.	Assurance	-0.9439	-0.6866	1.9944*
4.	Tangibles	-0.5337	-0.4077	0.8362
5.	Empathy	-1.0144	-0.0166	3.4563*

* Significant at five per cent level.

Customer Satisfaction Index Among the Convenience and Performance Seekers

The customer satisfaction towards the banks has been measured by the customers' attitude towards various related statements. It is summated with the help of an index called Customer Satisfaction Index. The Customer Satisfaction Index has been computed among the convenience and performance seekers, separately. The distribution of customers on the basis of their CSI is shown in Table 5.36. (*See Table on next page*)

The important CSI among the customers are 41 to 60 and 21 to 40 per cent which constitute 42.86 and 26.81 per cent to their respective total. The customers with the CSI of above 80 per cent constitutes 11.08 per cent of the total. The important CSI among the convenience seekers are 21 to 40 and 41 to 60 per cent which constitute 39.59 and 25.50 per cent to their respective total. Among the performance seekers, the two important CSI are 48.31 and 22.78 per cent of their respective total. The customer satisfaction among the performance seekers is relatively better among the performance seekers than among the convenience seekers.

Table 5.36: Customer Satisfaction Index (CSI) Among the Customers

Sl. No.	CSI (in per cent)	Number of Customers		Total
		CSR	PSR	
1.	Less than 21	23	44	67
2.	21-40	59	108	167
3.	41-60	38	229	267
4.	61-80	18	51	69
5.	Above 80	11	42	53
	Total	**149**	**474**	**623**

Impact of SERVPERF Scale of SQFs on CSI Among Convenience and Performance Seekers

The impact of perception on SQFs on the customers satisfaction among the convenience and performance seekers has been examined with the help of multiple regression analysis. The fitted regression model is

$$Y = a + b_1X_1 + b_2X_2 + b_3X_3 + b_4X_4 + b_5X_5 + e$$

where

Y – Customer Satisfaction Index among the customers

$X_1 \ldots X_5$ – Perception score on SQFs

$B_1 \ldots b_5$ – Regression coefficient of independent variables

a – Intercept and

e – Error term

Table 5.37: Impact of SERVPERF Scale of SQFS on CSI

Sl. No.	SQFs	Regression Coefficients among	
		CSR	PSR
1.	Reliability	0.0869	0.3145*
2.	Responsiveness	0.1142	0.2891*
3.	Assurance	0.0911	0.1446*
4.	Tangibles	0.2426*	0.0688
5.	Empathy	0.1442*	0.1133
	Constant	0.8969	1.2148
	R^2	0.7862	0.8191
	F-Statistics	9.3669*	13.6864

* Significant at five per cent level.

The impact of perception on SQFs on the customer satisfaction among the convenience seekers are tangibles and empathy. A unit increase in the perception on tangibles and empathy results in an increase in customer satisfaction by 0.2426 and 0.1442 units respectively. The changes in the perception on the SQFs explain the changes in customers satisfaction to the extent of 78.62 per cent. The significantly influencing SQFs on the customer satisfaction among the performance seekers are reliability, responsiveness and assurance. A unit increase in the perception on the above said SQFs would result in an increase in customer satisfaction by 0.3145, 0.2891 and 0.1446 units respectively.

Discriminate SQFs Among the Convenience and Performance Seekers

The basic expectation from the banks among the convenience seekers is different from that of performance seekers. It is highly essential to identify the important discriminate SQFs among the two types of customers for some policy implications. The two group discriminate analysis has been administered to identify such SQFs. The scores of perception on SQFs have been included for the analysis. Initially, the mean difference among the two groups of customers, regarding all SQFs, its 't' statistics and its significance have been computed and presented in Table 5.38.

Table 5.38: Mean Difference and Discriminate Power of SQFS

Sl. No.	SQFs	Mean Score among		Mean difference	'T' statistics	P-Value	Wilk's Lambda
		CSR	PSR				
1.	Reliability	2.9194	3.3990	-0.4796	-1.9854	0.0501	0.1428
2.	Responsiveness	2.7138	3.4367	-0.7229	-2.6339	0.0143	0.3811
3.	Assurance	2.5066	3.3546	-0.8480	-2.8411	0.0066	0.1317
4.	Tangibles	3.1481	2.9698	0.1783	0.5768	0.3314	0.4548
5.	Empathy	3.2021	3.8490	-0.6469	-2.1819	0.0365	0.2644

The higher mean difference among the two groups of customers has been noticed in the case of reliability, responsiveness, assurance and empathy since their respective mean differences are -0.4796, -0.7229, -0.8480 and -0.6469. The significant mean difference is also noticed in the above said four SQFs since their respective 't' statistics are significant at five per cent level. The performance seekers have a high rating on the above said four SQFs than the convenience seekers. The higher discriminate power of SQFs has been noticed in the case of assurance and reliability since their respective Wilk's Lambda are 0.1317 and 0.1428. The significant SQFs have been included for the establishment of two group discriminate function. The unstandardised procedure has been followed to establish the function. The estimated function is:

$$Z = -0.9385- 0.3468X_1-0.1861X_2+0.0419X_3-0.1844X_5$$

The relative contribution of the SQFs in the total discriminate score has been computed by the product of discriminate coefficient of the SQFs and their respective mean difference. The results are given in Table 5.39.

Table 5.39: Relative Importance of SQFS in Total Discriminate Score (TDS)

Sl. No.	SQFs	Canonical Discriminate Coefficient	Mean Difference	Product	Relative Contribution in TDS (in per cent)
1.	Reliability	-0.3468	-0.4796	0.1663	39.29
2.	Responsiveness	-0.1861	-0.7229	0.1345	31.78
3.	Assurance	0.0419	-0.8480	0.0355	08.40
4.	Empathy	-0.1344	-0.6469	0.0869	20.53
	Total			**0.4232**	**100.00**

Per cent of cases correctly classified: 68.33

The higher discriminate score is identified in the case of reliability and responsiveness since their respective discriminate coefficients are -0.3468 and -0.1861. It reveals that the above said two SQFs have a higher influence on the discriminate function. The higher relative contribution to the total discriminate score is identified in the case of the above two SQFs, since their respective relative contributions are 39.29 and 31.78 per cent. The estimated discriminate function correctly classifies the cases to the extent of 68.33 per cent. The analysis reveals that the important discriminate SQFs among the convenience and performance seekers are reliability and responsiveness. The performance seekers have high perception on the two SQFs than the convenience seekers.

Occupation Wise Segmentation Analysis

Occupation is one of the important profile of the customers. Depending upon the occupation of the customers, their requirements, expectations and perception on the SQFs may change. Usually, the business class expect convenient location and hours from the service providers. Apart from this, they may expect higher performance since their annual turnover is higher. These type of customers expect many value added services from the banks. Hence their perception on SQFs is an outcome of the comparison with other service providers. The perception on SQFs, among the professionals may differ from other groups of customers.

The expectation among the employees and the agriculturalists also differ from one another. The agriculturalists may have less knowledge and exposure on the banking environment and they may expect less from their bank. Hence, their perception on SQFs of commercial banks may be relatively higher than others. The agriculturalists may give more importance to the 'empathy' factor. If they are satisfied on the above said SQFs, they may said to be fully satisfied. But it is not the same situation among the other groups of customers. Hence, the present study has made an attempt to analyse the expectation and perception on SQFs among the agriculturists, employees and businessmen. The customers are classified into the above said three groups.

Customers' Perception on SQFs (Occupation-wise Analysis)

The SERVPERF scale on the five SQFs among the agriculturalists, employees and businessmen have been computed to compare the level of perception on the SQFs among the three groups of customers. The score on SQFs is derived from the mean score of the variables in each factor. The one way analysis of variance has been executed to analyse the significant difference among the three groups of customers regarding their SERVPERF scale on SQFs. (*See Table on next page*)

Table 5.40 explains the mean score of SERVPERF scale on SQFs among the three groups of customers and their respective 'F' statistics. The highly perceived SQFs among the agriculturalists are empathy and tangibles since their respective mean scores are 3.2341 and 3.0968 whereas among the employees, these SQFS are reliability and assurance since their respective mean scores are 3.2445 and 3.1089. The highly perceived SQFs among the businessmen are responsiveness and reliability since their respective mean scores are 3.7463 and 3.6661. Regarding the perception on SQFs, the significant difference among the three groups of customers has been identified in the case of reliability and responsiveness since their respective 'F' statistics are significant at five per cent level.

Table 5.40: Perception on SQFS (SERVPERF Scale) Among Different Groups of Customers Based on Occupation

Sl. No.	SQFs	Mean Score			F-Statistics
		Agricul-turalist	Employee	Business-men	
1.	Reliability	2.7184	3.2445	3.6661	3.8104*
2.	Responsiveness	3.0417	2.8141	3.7463	3.0621*
3.	Assurance	2.7211	3.1089	3.4519	2.1149
4.	Tangibles	3.0968	2.7144	3.1885	1.5803
5.	Empathy	3.2341	3.0365	3.5759	1.0447

* Significant at five per cent level.

SERVQUAL Scale on SQFs (Occupation Wise Analysis)

The SERVQUAL scale is the difference between the level of perception and expectation on SQFs among the customers. The study on SERVQUAL scale on SQFs is essential to make future policy implications to reduce the gap between the level of expectation and perception on SQFs. In the present study, the SERVQUAL scale on SQFs among the agriculturalists, employees and businessmen has been computed separately. The one way analysis of variance has been applied to find out the significant difference among them.

Table 5.41: SERVQUAL Scale Among Different Types of Customers Based on Occupation

Sl. No.	SQFs	Mean Score among			F-Statistics
		Agricul-turalists	Employees	Business-men	
1.	Reliability	-0.7284	-0.3732	-0.4410	2.9917*
2.	Responsiveness	-0.4795	-0.8083	-0.3571	3.1408*
3.	Assurance	-0.6235	-0.7828	-0.7997	1.0223
4.	Tangibles	0.0326	-0.6200	-0.5903	3.2149
5.	Empathy	-0.3846	-0.5581	-0.8511	3.0816*

* Significant at five per cent level.

Table 5.41 illustrates the mean score of SERVQUAL scale on SQFs and its respective 'F' statistics. The higher SERVQUAL scale among the agriculturalists is identified in the case of reliability and assurance since their respective mean scores are -0.7284 and -0.6235 whereas among the employees, these are responsiveness and assurance since their respective mean scores are -0.8083 and -0.7828. Among the businessmen, it is identified in the case of empathy and assurance since their mean scores are -0.8511 and -0.7997 respectively. Regarding the SERVQUAL scale on SQFs, the significant difference among the three occupational groups of customers has been noticed in the case of reliability, responsiveness and empathy since their respective 'F' statistics are significant at five per cent level.

Customer Satisfaction Index Among the Customers

The customer satisfaction among the three groups of customers has been examined with the help of the Customers Satisfaction Index (CSI). The CSI reveals the overall attitude of the customers towards the banking facilities availed by them. The CSI in the present study is confined to less than 21 per cent, 21 to 40, 41 to 60, 61 to 80 and above 80 per cent. The distribution of customers on the basis of their CSI is given in Table 5.42.

Table 5.42: Customer Satisfaction Index (CSI) Among the Customers

Sl. No.	CSI (in per cent)	Number of Customers			Total
		Agricul-turalists	Employees	Business-men	
1.	Less than 21	18	39	51	108
2.	21-40	29	27	67	123
3.	41-60	41	49	69	159
4.	61-80	47	58	48	153
5.	Above 80	27	27	26	80
	Total	**162**	**200**	**261**	**623**

The important CSIs among the customers are 41 to 60 and 61 to 80 per cent which constitute 25.52 and 24.56 per cent to their respective total. The customers with an index of above 80 per cent constitutes 12.84 per cent of the total. The important index among the agriculturalists are 61 to 80 and 41 to 60 per cent which constitute 29.01 and 25.30 per cent to their respective total. Among the employees, these two are 61 to 80 and 41 to 60 per cent which constitute 29.00 and 24.50 per cent to their respective total. Among the businessmen, the important CSI are 41 to 60 and 21 to 40 since they constitute 26.44 and 25.67 per cent to their respective total. The analysis reveals that the agriculturalists are more satisfied compared to the other two groups whereas the businessmen are more dissatisfied compared to the other two groups.

Impact of SERVPERF Scale on SQFs on CSI

The impact of SERVPERF scales on SQFs on the CSI among the agriculturalists, employees and businessmen has been analysed with the help of multiple regression analysis. The CSI among the customers is treated as the score of the dependent variables whereas the SERVPERF scale on SQFs is treated as the score of independent variables. The Ordinary Least Square (OLS) method has been followed to identify the degree of influence of SQFs on the CSI among the three groups of customers separately. The results are shown in Table 5.43.

Table 5.43: Impact of SERVPERF of SQFS on CSI

Sl. No.	SQFs	Regression Co-efficients among Customers		
		Agricul-turalists	Employees	Business-men
1.	Reliability	0.1427*	0.1819*	0.2424*
2.	Responsiveness	0.0933	0.1502*	0.1761*
3.	Assurance	-0.0438	0.1617*	0.0669
4.	Tangibles	0.1081	0.0961	0.1104
5.	Empathy	0.1884*	-0.0539	0.2478*
	Constant	0.9134	1.2441	1.8569
	R2	0.7872	0.8194	0.8646
	F-Statistics	8.1816*	10.3326*	12.8603*

* Significant at five per cent level.

Among the agriculturalists, the significantly influencing SERVPERF scale of SQFs on the CSI are reliability and empathy since their respective regression coefficients are significant at five per cent level. A unit increase in the SERVPERF scale on reliability and empathy will result in an increase in CSI by 0.1427 and 0.1884 units respectively. The changes in the SERVPERF scale on SQFs explain the changes in CSI to the extent of 78.72 per cent.

The significantly influencing SERVPERF scale of SQFs on CSI, among the employees are reliability, responsiveness and assurance. A unit increase in the SERVPERF scale on the above said SQFs will result in an increase in CSI by 0.1819, 0.1502 and 0.1617 units respectively. The changes in

SERVPERF scale on SQFs explain the changes in CSI among the employees to the extent of 81.94 per cent. Among the businessmen, a unit increase in the SERVPERF scale on reliability, responsiveness and empathy will result in an increase in CSI by 0.2424, 0.1761 and 0.2478 units respectively. The changes in the SERVPERF scale on SQFs, among the businessmen, explain the changes in CSI to the extent of 86.46 per cent. The analysis reveals that the businessmen are highly influenced by the SERVPERF scale on SQFs compared to the other two groups of customers.

Discriminate SQFs among the Three Occupational Groups of Customers

The customers with different occupational background may perceive the service quality in commercial banks in different ways since their level of knowledge, awareness and expectations from the banks are different. The present analysis has made an attempt to identify the important discriminate SQFs among the three occupational groups, with the help of multiple discriminate analysis. Initially, the mean score of perception on SQFs among the three groups of customers, its 't' statistics with its statistical significance and Wilk's Lambda have been computed and presented in Table 5.44. (*See Table on next page*)

The significant difference among the three occupational group of customers has been identified in the case of reliability and responsiveness since their respective 't' statistics are significant at five per cent level. The most perceived SQFs among the agriculturalists and employees are empathy and reliability since their respective mean scores are 3.2341 and 3.2445. Among the businessmen, it is identified in the case of responsiveness. Low levels of Wilk's Lambda have been noticed in the case reliability and responsiveness since their respective Wilk's Lambda coefficient is 0.1048 and 0.1631.

Table 5.44: Mean Difference and

Sl. No.	SQFs	Mean Score among Customers			F-Statistics	P-Value	Wilk's Lambda
		Agriculturalist	Employee	Businessmen			
1.	Reliability	2.7184	3.2445	3.6661	3.8104	0.0296	0.1048
2.	Responsiveness	3.0417	2.8141	3.7463	3.0621	0.0451	0.1631
3.	Assurance	2.7211	3.1089	3.4519	2.1149	0.0739	0.2411
4.	Tangibles	3.0968	2.7144	3.1885	1.5803	0.1641	0.3916
5.	Empathy	3.2341	3.0365	3.5759	1.0447	0.2462	0.2862

Canonical Discriminate Function

Based on occupation, the customers are classified into three groups namely agriculturalists, employees and businessmen. The perception scores on the five SQFs among the three groups of customers have been included for multi-discriminate analysis. Since the number of customer groups are three, the multi-discriminate analysis can generate a minimum of only two discriminate functions. The reliability and validity of these two functions have been analysed with the help of eigen value, per cent of the explained variance and canonical correlation. The results are shown in Table 5.45. *(See Table on next page)*

The eigen value of the first function is 4.2917 and this accounts for 92.03 per cent of the explained variance. Because of the high eigen value, the first function is declared as superior over the other functions. The second function has a smaller eigen value of 0.4486 and accounts for only 7.97 per cent of the explained variance. The '0' below after function indicates that no function has been removed. The value of Wilk's Lambda is 0.1433. This transforms to a chi-square of 46.1439, which is significant at zero per cent level. Thus the two functions together significantly discriminate the three occupational groups of customers. However, Wilk's Lambda of the second function is 0.8696 which is not significant at five per cent level. Therefore, the second function is declared to be not contributing significantly to the group differences.

Table 5.45: Canonical Discriminate Function

Function	Eigen Value	Per cent of Variance	Cumulative per cent of Variance	Canonical Correlation	After Function	Wilk's Lambda Value	Chi-Square	P-Value
1.	4.2917	92.03	92.03	0.8149	0	0.1433	46.1439	0.0000
2.	0.4486	7.97	100.00	0.2432	1	0.8696	3.1468	0.3919

Discriminate Coefficient of the Various SQFs

The multi-discriminate analysis generates two discriminate functions. These two functions reveal the discriminate coefficients of the SQFs among the three occupational groups of customers. Since the first function is proved to be the superior one, that function alone is taken for the interpretation. The discriminate coefficients of SQFs in Function-1 and Function-2 are illustrated in Table 5.46.

Table 5.46: Standardised Canonical Discriminate Function Coefficients

Sl. No.	SQFs	Functions	
		Function-1	Function 2
1.	Reliability	0.2469	0.0811
2.	Responsiveness	0.1333	0.1022
3.	Assurance	-0.1086	0.0986
4.	Tangibles	0.1211	0.2455
5.	Empathy	0.3341	0.1371
	Per cent of cases correctly classified	88.26	21.67

The first function correctly estimates the cases to the extent of 88.26 per cent. The higher discriminate coefficients are identified in the case of empathy and reliability since their respective discriminate coefficients are 0.3341 and 0.2469. The analysis reveals that the three occupational groups of customers are discriminated, mainly on the basis of empathy and reliability. Hence, the bank managers should carefully analyse the components of these two factors, before offering their service to the different occupational groups of customers.

Experience Wise Segmentation Analysis

The years of experience in banking activities, among the customers is one of their important profiles. The years of experience among the customers plays an important role in their expectation and perception on the SQFs. The experienced customers may have more awareness, knowledge and analytical skill, to evaluate the service quality offered by the banks. Since, they are highly capable of comparing the services and service quality of the present bank with other competitive banks, their level of expectation and perception on SQFs may be influenced by their analysis. At the same time, the less experienced customers' knowledge and exposure on the banking environment is relatively less. Hence, they may not expect more from their banks and they are easily satisfied with their bankers in all aspects. The bank managers have to analyse the years of experience among the customers, before they consider any policy implications. Hence, the present analysis focuses on the level of expectation, and perception on SQFs, among the different experienced groups of customers. In the present study, the customers are classified into less experienced, experienced and highly experienced groups.

SERVPERF Scale on SQFs Among Customers with Different Experience Levels

The perception on SQFs is equally important for their level of expectation on SQFs among the customers, since it will provide information for the future policy implications. The present analysis has made an attempt on analyzing the level of perception on SQFs among different experienced customers, with the help of its mean score of perception on SQFs. It is derived from the mean score of the perception, on the variables included in each factor. The mean score of perception on the SQFs and their respective 'F' statistics are illustrated in Table 5.47

Table 5.47: Perception on SQF (SERVPERF Scale) Among the Customers

Sl. No.	SQFs	Mean Score among Customers			F-Statistics
		LED	ED	HED	
1.	Reliability	3.6817	3.4149	2.9524	3.0044*
2.	Responsiveness	3.6503	3.3814	2.9511	2.9996*
3.	Assurance	3.3084	3.2041	3.0201	0.9197
4.	Tangibles	3.1496	3.0684	2.8859	0.8024
5.	Empathy	3.7502	3.6717	2.7199	3.2191*

The less experienced customers have more perception on the SQFs than the other two groups of experienced customers since their mean score of the perception on SQFs is greater than the relevant mean score among the other two groups. The highly perceived SQFs among the less experienced customers are empathy and reliability since their mean scores are 3.7502 and 3.6817 respectively. Among the experienced customers, these SQFs are also empathy and reliability but their respective mean scores are 3.6717 and 3.4149. Among the highly experienced customers, these SQFs are assurance and reliability since their mean scores are 3.0201 and 2.9524 respectively. Regarding the perception on SQFs, the significant difference among the three groups of customers has been noticed in the perception on reliability, responsiveness and empathy, since their respective 'F' statistics are significant at five per cent level.

SERVQUAL scale on the SQFs among Customers with Different Levels of Experience

The deviation between the level of perception and level of expectation on SQFs among the customers is examined with the help of the SERVQUAL scale. The negative SERVQUAL scale indicates that the level of perception on SQFs among the customers, is not upto the expectation on SQFs. It is an imperative area for the marketers to reduce the gap between these two levels. The present analysis reveals the mean score of SERVQUAL scale on SQFs and their respective 'F' statistics in Table 5.48.

Table 5.48: SERVQUAL Scale Among the Customers with Different Levels of Experience

Sl. No.	SQFs	Mean Score among Customers			F-Statistics
		LED	ED	HED	
1.	Reliability	0.2256	-0.1972	-1.1594	3.8814*
2.	Responsiveness	-0.1701	-0.1275	-1.3087	3.6026*
3.	Assurance	-0.3035	-0.4302	-1.3039	3.2171*
4.	Tangibles	-0.0585	-0.2557	-0.8165	3.0696*
5.	Empathy	0.2361	0.0311	-1.7043	3.5044*

* Significant at five per cent level.

The positive SERVQUAL scale is identified in empathy among the less experienced and experienced customers since the level of perception on empathy is greater than their level of expectation among the above said two groups of customers. But it is negative among the highly experienced customers. In the SQF of reliability, the mean of SERVQUAL scale is positive among the less experienced customers whereas among the remaining two groups of customers, it is negative. In all other cases, there is a negative SERVQUAL scale. It infers that the level of perception on SQFs are not upto the level of expectation on SQFs, especially, responsiveness, assurance and tangibles among all the three groups of customers. Regarding the SERVQUAL scale, there is a significant difference among the three groups of customers since their respective 'F' statistics are significant at five per cent level.

Customer Satisfaction Index Among the Three Groups

The customer satisfaction towards banking, among the customers has been measured by relevant statements. The customers are asked to rate these statements at five point scale. The scores of these statements, among the customers, have been taken into account to establish the Customer Satisfaction Index (CSI). The CSI in the present study is confined to less than 21 per cent, 21 to 40, 41 to 60, 61 to 80 and above 80 per cent. The distribution of customers on the basis of CSI is shown in Table 5.49.

Table 5.49: Customer Satisfaction Index (CSI) Among the Customers

Sl. No.	CSI (in per cent)	Number of Customers			Total
		LED	ED	HED	
1.	Less than 21	13	21	27	61
2.	21-40	22	36	49	107
3.	41-60	26	103	98	227
4.	61-80	30	65	46	141
5.	Above 80	27	36	24	87
	Total	**118**	**261**	**244**	**623**

The important CSIs among the customers are 41 to 60 and 61 to 80 per cent which constitute 36.44 and 22.63 per cent to their respective total. The customers, with an index of above 80 per cent constitutes 13.96 per cent of the total. The important CSIs among the less experienced customers are 61 to 80 and above 80 per cent which constitute 25.42 and 22.88 per cent to their respective total whereas among the experienced customers, these two are 41 to 60 and 61 to 80 per cent constituting 39.46 and 24.90 per cent to their respective total. Among the highly experienced customers, these are 41 to 60 and 21 to 60 per cent which constitute 40.16 and 20.08 per cent to their respective total. In total, the highly experienced customers are less satisfied than the other two types of customers.

Impact of SERVPERF Scale of SQFs on CSI

The impact of SERVPERF scale of SQFs on CSI among the three groups of customers, has been examined, with the help of multiple regression analysis. The Ordinary Least Square method has been executed to establish this function. The impact analysis has been examined to identify the relative importance of the perception on each SQFs, on the overall customer satisfaction, for future policy implications. The results are given in Table 5.50.

Table 5.50: Impact of SERVPERF Scale on SQFS on CSI

Sl. No.	SQFs	Regression Co-efficient among Customers		
		LED	ED	HED
1.	Reliability	0.1819*	0.2106*	0.3149*
2.	Responsiveness	0.1024	0.0882	0.2908*
3.	Assurance	0.2669*	0.1914*	0.0414
4.	Tangibles	0.2994*	0.0911	0.1023
5.	Empathy	0.1448*	0.1446*	0.1818*
	Constant	1.2496	1.0244	1.4329
	R^2	0.7961	0.7336	0.7696
	F-Statistics	10.3893*	9.0981*	10.1142*

* Significant at five per cent level.

Among the less experienced customers, the significantly influencing SQFs on the CSI are reliability, assurance, tangibles and empathy. A unit increase in the perception on the above said SQFs would result in an increase in CSI by 0.1819, 0.2669, 0.2994 and 0.1448 units respectively. The changes in the perception on SQFs explain the changes in CSI to the extent of 79.61 per cent. Among the experienced customers, these SQFs are reliability, assurance and empathy. A unit increase in the SERVQUAL scale on the above said SQFs will result in an increase in CSI by 0.2106, 0.1914 and 0.1446 units respectively.

Among the highly experienced customers, the significantly influencing SERVPERF scale of SQFs on the CSI are reliability, responsiveness and empathy. A unit increase in the perception on the above said SQFs would result in an increase in CSI by 0.3149, 0.2908 and 0.1818 units respectively. The changes in the perception on the SQFs, explain the changes in CSI among the customers to the extent of 76.96 per cent. The analysis reveals that the changes in the perception on SQFs, explain more on the changes in CSI among the less experienced than the other two groups. The main influencing SQFs on the CSI among the less experienced, experienced and highly experienced customers are tangibles, reliability and reliability respectively.

Discriminate Service Quality Factors Among the Three Experience Groups of Customers

The customers with different years of experience in banking may be different in their level of expectation, perception and comparison on the service quality of the commercial banks. The experienced customers may have more knowledge in banking and also they may expect more from their bankers. It is not easy to satisfy the experienced customers as in the case of freshers. Hence, bankers have to deliver superior service quality to them. At the same time, the less experienced customers are having less loyalty towards their banks. Hence, they may easily switch over to other banks if they are not satisfied with the present banks.

It is highly imperative to identify the important discriminate service quality factors among the three experienced groups of customers, for some policy implications. The mean score of SQFs, its 'F' statistics with level of significance and Wilk's Lambda have been examined and shown in Table 5.51.

Table 5.51: Mean Difference and Discriminate Power of SQFS

Sl. No.	SQFs	Mean Score among Customers			F-Statistics	P-Value	Wilk's Lambda
		LED	ED	HED			
1.	Reliability	3.6817	3.4149	2.9524	3.0044	0.0299	0.1209
2.	Responsiveness	3.6503	3.3814	2.9511	2.9996	0.0306	0.1817
3.	Assurance	3.3084	3.2041	3.0201	0.9197	0.1968	0.4144
4.	Tangibles	3.1496	3.0684	2.8859	0.8024	0.2147	0.3908
5.	Empathy	3.7502	3.6717	2.7199	3.2191	0.0139	0.1646

The significant mean difference among the three groups of customers has been identified in their perception on reliability, responsiveness and empathy, since their respective 't' statistics are significant at five per cent level. Higher discriminate power is noticed in reliability, empathy and responsiveness since their Wilk's Lambda are 0.1209, 0.1646 and 0.1817 respectively. It infers that the above said three SQFs are have more discriminate power to discriminate the three levels of experienced customers.

Canonical Discriminate Function

The number of groups, included for the analysis is three. Hence the multi-discriminate analysis can generate only two discriminate functions. The reliability and validity of these two functions are exhibited with the help of its eigen value, per cent of variance, canonical correlation and the Wilk's Lambda in Table 5.52.

Table 5.52: Canonical Discriminsate Functions

Function	Eigen Value	Per cent of Variance	Cumulative per cent of Variance	Canonical Correlation	After Function	Wilk's Lambda	Chi-Square Value	P-Value
1.	5.1922	82.86	82.86	0.8446	0	0.1086	51.0824	0.0000
2.	0.8692	17.14	100.00	0.1241	1	0.8429	2.9196	0.6148

The eigen value of the first function is 5.1922 and this accounts for 82.86 per cent of explained variance. Because of the high eigen value, the first function is declared as superior to the other functions. The second function has a smaller eigen value of 0.8692 and accounts for only 17.14 per cent of the explained variance. The '0' below after function indicates that no function has been removed. The value of Wilk's Lambda is 0.1086. This transforms to a chi-square of 51.0824, which is significant at zero per cent level. Thus the two functions together, significantly discriminate the three levels of experience of the customers. However, Wilk's Lambda of the second function is 0.8429 which is not significant at five per cent level. Therefore, the second function alone is declared to be not contributing to the group differences.

Discriminate Coefficients of the Various SQFs

Eventhough, the multi discriminate analysis generates two functions, the first function alone is taken for the interpretation since it has been proved as superior to another and it is also statistically significant. The discriminate coefficients of function-1 and function-2 are summarized in Table 5.53. (*See Table on next page*)

The first function correctly estimates the cases to the extent of 73.37 per cent, compared to function-2 which estimates the cases correctly to the extent of 11.47 per cent only. The higher discriminate coefficients of SQFs in function-1 are identified in the case of reliability and tangibles since their respective discriminate coefficients are 0.3408 and -

0.2969. The study infers that the important discriminate SQFs among the three levels of experience of the customers, are reliability and tangibles. Hence, the bank managers have to concentrate on the above said two SQFs in their future policy decisions.

Table 5.53: Standardised Canonical Discriminate Function Coefficients

Sl. No.	SQFs	Functions	
		Function-1	Function-2
1.	Reliability	0.3408	0.1081
2.	Responsiveness	0.2149	0.0949
3.	Assurance	-0.1084	0.2842
4.	Tangibles	-0.2969	-0.1911
5.	Empathy	0.1441	0.3861
	Per cent of cases correctly classified	73.37	11.47

REFERENCES

1. Bowen, J.W and Hedges, R.B (1993), "Increasing Service Quality in retail banking", *Journal of Retail Banking*, 15(2), pp. 21-28.
2. Belch, G.E and Belch, M.A (1993), *Introduction to Advertising and Promotion*, 2nd ed., Irvin, Homewood, IL.
3. Kotler, P and Armstrong, G (1991), *Principles of Marketing*, 5th ed., Prentice-Hall, Eaglewood Cliffs, NJ.
4. Kotler, P. and Armstrong, G (1991), Principles of Marketing, 5th ed., Prentice-Hall, Englewood cliffs, NJ.
5. Plank, R.E., Greene, R.C. and Greene, J.N (1994), "Understanding which Spouse makes financial decisions", *Journal of Retail Banking*, 16(1), pp. 21-26.
6. Thompson, A.M and Kaminski, P (1993), "Psychographic and Lifestyle Antecedents of Service Quality Expectations: A Segmentation Approach", *Journal of Services Marketing*, 7(4), pp. 53-61.
7. Welster, C (1989), "Can consumers be Segmented on the Basis of Their Service Quality Expectation?", *Journal of Services Marketing*, 3(2), pp. 35.

Summary of Findings Conclusion and Policy Implications

The present study is accomplished in three stages. The first stage focuses on the profile of the customers in selected commercial banks, the service quality in commercial banks and the customers' satisfaction towards banking. It is followed by the level of expectation on service quality of commercial banks among different groups of customers and the discriminate demographic profile variables related to the expectation on service quality of commercial banks. In the third stage, the customer segmentation analysis has been done regarding the level of perception on service quality in commercial banks.

The specific objectives of this study were:

(i) To exhibit the profile of the customers in selected banks;

(ii) To identify the service quality factors and customers' satisfaction towards banking;

(iii) To analyse the level of expectation on service quality in commercial banks.

(iv) To identify the role of demographic profile of the customers in their expectation on service quality of commercial banks.

(v) To examine the perception on service quality in commercial banks among different customer segments.

(vi) To evaluate the impact of perception on service quality in commercial banks on the customers' satisfaction and

(vii) To identify the important discriminate service quality factors among the different group of customers.

The concepts and the methodology were formulated according to the objectives of the study, with the help of comprehensive reviews of previous studies. The secondary data about the commercial banks were collected from relevant journals and records.

For primary data, 112 public sector banks, 25 private sector banks and 6 new private sector banks in Kanyakumari district were included for the present study. From each bank, 10 customers were selected as samples for the study. The total sample size came to 1430. These sample were distributed among the different strata in the population according to the proportion of the banks to the total number of banks. Hence, the applied sampling procedure is stratified proportionate random sampling. The response rate among the consumers is only 43.56 per cent. Hence the included sample size of the present study is 623 customers.

The collected data were analysed with the help of appropriate tools to examine the service quality factors, customers satisfaction towards banks, level of expectation and perception on various service quality factors among different customer segments and also the discriminate service quality factors in each customer segment. The various findings of the present study are summarized below:

The important age group among the customers is 25 to 45 years. The most important age group among the customers in Public Sector Banks is 36 to 45 years whereas in Private Sector and New Private Banks, these are 25 to 35 years and less than 25 years respectively. The important gender among the customers is male.

The important nativity of the customers is urban. The dominant levels of education among the customers are undergraduation and post graduation. The most important level of education among the customers in all three groups of banks is undergraduation. The important monthly income category among the customers is above Rs.30,000. It is followed by Rs. 20,001 to 25,000 and Rs. 25,000 to 30,000.

The dominant occupations among the customers are business and private employment. The most important occupation among the customers in all three groups of banks is 'business'. Majority of the customers are having an experience of 10 to 13 years with their banks which is followed by above 17 years of experience.

The type of the customers is classified with the help of nine variables. The nine variables are narrated into two factors namely 'performance' and 'convenience'. The reliability and validity of the variables in each factor are confirmed by the convergent validity and composite reliability. The customers in New Private Sector Banks are highly seeking the 'performance' of the banks whereas in Public Sector Banks, the customers are seeking 'convenience'. In total, the important type of customers are performance seekers in all three groups of banks. But the number of convenience seekers is higher in Public Sector Banks.

Totally, 35 service quality variables have been included to find out the important service quality factors in commercial banks. Out of the 35 variables, 10 variables have been excluded by exploratory factor analysis, since their respective factor loadings are less than 0.4 or the higher factor loadings are associated with more than one factor narrated by the factor analysis. Finally, the factor analysis results in five important Service Quality Factors (SQFs) namely reliability, responsiveness, assurance, tangibles and empathy.

All the five SQFs consist of five SQ variables each. The factors are reliability, responsiveness, assurance, tangibles and empathy. The validity and reliability of the SQFs are confirmed with the help of confirmatory factor analysis. The convergent validity and composite reliability of the variables in each factor have been verified. Since the inter correlation between the service quality factors is of low degree and the correlation coefficients are not significant at five per cent level, the discriminate validity is also confirmed between the SQFs.

The highly expected SQFs among the customers in Public Sector Banks (PSBs) are 'empathy' and 'assurance' whereas in Private Sector Banks (PrsBs) there are 'responsiveness' and 'empathy'. In the case of New Private Sector Banks (NPrSBs), these are 'assurance' and 'empathy'. Regarding the level of expectations, there is no significant difference among the customers of the three groups of banks.

The highly perceived SQFs among the customers in PSBs are 'responsiveness' and 'empathy' whereas among the customers in PrSBs, these are 'responsiveness' and 'reliability'. Among the customers in NPrSBs, these are 'empathy' and 'reliability'. Regarding the level of perception on SQFs, the significant difference among the customers of the three groups of banks have been identified in their perception on reliability, responsiveness, assurance and empathy.

The SERVQUAL scale indicates the difference between the perception and expectation on SQFs. In all five SQFs, the SERVQUAL scale is identified as negative among all customers of the three group of banks. It infers that the customers in all the three groups of banks are not satisfied upto their level of expectation. Regarding the SERVQUAL scale, the significant difference among the three groups of customers has been noticed in the case of reliability, responsiveness, assurance and empathy.

The customers' satisfaction towards the banks have been measured with the help of twelve statements. The variables are narrated into two factors namely employee and bank. The variables included in employee and bank factors reveals the validity and reliability through its convergent validity, reliability coefficient and composite reliability. Since there is no discriminate validity between the two factors in customer satisfaction, the score of the statements related to customer satisfaction is summated with the help of an index called Customer Satisfaction Index (CSI). The important CSI among the customers are 41 to 60 and 21 to 40 per cent. The most important CSI among the customer in PSBs is 21 to 40 per cent whereas in PrSBs and NPrSBs, they are 61 to 80 and above 80 per cent. The analysis reveals that customer satisfaction is higher among customers in NPrSBs than those in PrSBs and PSBs.

The significantly and positively influencing SERVPERF scale of SQFs on customer satisfaction, among the customers in PSBs are 'reliability' and 'empathy' whereas in PrSBs, these are 'reliability', 'responsiveness', 'tangibles' and 'empathy'. Among the customers in NPrSBs, these are all the five SQFs. The important discriminate SQFs among the three groups of banks, regarding their perception on SQFs are 'empathy' and 'assurance'. The customers in PSBs rate the empathy at a very low level whereas the customers in NPrSBs, it is rated high. The same trend is identified in the perception on 'assurance'.

'Nativity' is one of the important discriminators of the service quality expectation among the customers. The level of expectation on all the five SQFs significantly differ among the urban and rural customers. The highly expected SQFs among the urban customers are 'empathy' and 'assurance' whereas among the rural customers, they are 'responsiveness' and 'reliability'. The urban customers expect more from their banks than their counterparts.

The significant mean difference among the urban and rural customers has been noticed in the level of expectation on all the five SQFs. Higher discriminate power is identified in the case of empathy and assurance factors. The important discriminate SQFs among the urban and rural customers are 'empathy' and 'reliability' regarding their level of expectation from banks.

Based on the age of the customers, they are classified into youngsters, middle aged and aged. The level of expectation on SQFs among the youngsters is greater than the level of expectation on SQFs among other two groups except in 'empathy' factor. The highly expected SQFs among the youngsters are 'assurance' and 'reliability' whereas among the middle aged, these are 'empathy' and 'reliability'. Among the aged, these are 'empathy' and 'assurance'.

Regarding the level of expectation among the three groups of customers, significant difference is identified in the level of expectation on reliability, responsiveness and assurance. The higher discriminate power is noticed in the case of reliability and assurance. The important discriminate SQFs among the three age groups of customers are 'reliability' and 'responsiveness' which are very high among youngsters compared to the other two age-group of customers.

Regarding the level of expectation on SQFs, significant difference among male and female customers has been identified in the case of reliability, responsiveness, tangibles and empathy. The female customers are found to be expecting more than their counterparts. The highly expected SQFs among the male customers are 'assurance' and 'empathy' whereas among the female customers, these are 'reliability' and 'empathy'. Regarding the level of expectation, the important discriminate SQFs among the male and female customers have been noticed in the case of 'empathy' and 'reliability' and the female customers are expecting more than the male customers.

By the level of education, the customers are classified into less educated, educated and highly educated. Regarding the level of expectation on SQFs, the significant difference among the three educated groups of customers have been identified in the level of expectation on reliability, responsiveness and tangibles. The highly expected SQFs among the less educated and educated customers are 'empathy' and 'assurance' whereas among the highly educated customers, these SQFs are 'reliability' and 'assurance'.

The higher discriminate power of the SQF is identified in the case of 'reliability' and 'tangibles'. The important discriminate SQFs among the three educated groups of customers are 'reliability' and 'empathy'. Reliability is highly expected by the highly educated whereas 'empathy' is highly expected by the less educated customers.

The highly expected SQFs among the Less Income Groups (LIGs) are 'empathy' and 'assurance' whereas among the Middle Income Groups (MIGs), these are 'assurance' and 'responsiveness'. Among the Higher Income Groups (HIGs), these are 'assurance' and 'reliability'. In total, the HIGs are found to be expecting more SQF from their service providers than the other two income groups.

Regarding the level of expectation on SQFs, the significant difference among the three income groups of customers has been noticed in the level of expectation on 'reliability', 'responsiveness' and 'assurance'. The higher discriminate power of the SQFs is noticed in the case of responsiveness and reliability. The important discriminate

SQFs among the three income groups are 'reliability' and 'responsiveness' which are very high among the HIGs compared to the other income groups.

Based on benefit segmentation, the customers are classified into convenience seekers and performance seekers. The highly expected SQFs among the convenience seekers are 'empathy' and 'tangibles' whereas among the performance seekers, these two are 'assurance' and 'responsiveness'. Regarding the level of expectation, the significant difference among the two groups of customers has been identified in their level of expectation on responsiveness, reliability and assurance. The higher discriminate power of SQFs is noticed in the case of responsiveness and empathy. The important discriminate SQFs among the convenience and performance seekers are reliability and responsiveness which are higher among the performance seekers.

Based on the occupation of the customers, they are classified into agriculturalists, employees and businessmen. The highly expected SQFs among the agriculturalists are empathy and responsiveness whereas among the employees, these are assurance and responsiveness. Among the businessmen, these two SQFs are empathy and assurance. Regarding the level of expectation on SQFs, the significant difference among the three groups of customers has been identified in their level of expectation on reliability, assurance, tangibles and empathy. The higher discriminate power of SQF is noticed in the case of empathy and assurance. The important discriminate SQFs among the three groups of customers are empathy and reliability. The empathy and reliability factors are highly expected by businessmen than the other two groups of customers.

Based on banking experience, the customers are classified into Less Experienced (LED), Experienced (ED) and Highly Experienced (HED). The highly expected SQFs among the LED and ED are assurance and empathy whereas among the HED, these are empathy and assurance. Regarding the level of expectation, the significant difference among the three experienced groups of customers is identified in their level of expectation on all SQFs. The higher discriminate power of SQF is noticed in the case of responsiveness and assurance. The important discriminate SQFs among the three groups of customers are assurance and responsiveness and these are higher among the highly experienced than the other two groups.

The highly perceived SQFs among the urban customers are empathy and reliability whereas among the rural customers, these are assurance and responsiveness. The level of perception on SQFs among the rural customers is less than the level of perception among the urban customers. The significant difference between the urban and rural customers has been identified in the perception on reliability, responsiveness and empathy.

The level of perception of SQFs is less than the level of expectation on SQFs among the urban and rural customers except in tangibles. Regarding tangibles, the rural customers' perception is higher than their level of expectation. Regarding the SERVQUAL scale, the significant difference among the urban and rural customers has been noticed in the case of assurance, tangibles and empathy.

The rural customers show higher level of satisfaction than the urban customers. The significantly and positively influencing SQFs on the customer satisfaction among the urban customers are reliability, responsiveness and empathy whereas among the rural customers, these SQFs are reliability, responsiveness, tangibles and empathy. Regarding the perception on SQFs, the important discriminate SQFs among the urban and rural customers are responsiveness, reliability and empathy and the urban customers show more perception on the above said SQFs than the rural customers.

The highly perceived SQFs among the youngsters are assurance and reliability whereas among middle aged customers, these are empathy and responsiveness. Among the aged customers, these SQFs are empathy and tangibles. Regarding the perception on SQFs, the significant difference among the three age groups of customers has been identified in the perception on assurance and empathy.

The SERVQUAL scale on SQFs reveals that the SERVQUAL scale is negative in all SQFs among all the three groups of customers except in 'tangibles' factor especially among the aged customers. The analysis reveals that the customers are not satisfied upto their level of expectation on SQFs. Regarding the SERVQUAL scale on SQFs, the significant difference among the three age groups of customers has been identified in the case of reliability, responsiveness, tangibles and empathy.

The customers' satisfaction towards banks is higher among the aged customers than among the other two groups of customers. The significantly and positively influencing SQFs on customer satisfaction, among the youngsters are reliability and assurance whereas among the middle aged, these are responsiveness, assurance and empathy. Among the aged customers, these SQFs are reliability, responsiveness, tangibles and empathy.

The higher discriminate power of SQF is noticed in the case of empathy and assurance. The important discriminate SQFs among the three age groups of customers are empathy and tangibles. The aged customers perceive more on these two SQFs whereas the youngsters show very low perception on these two SQFs.

The female customers show more perception on SQFs compared to male customers. The highly perceived SQFs among the male customers are empathy and reliability whereas among the female customers, these are responsiveness and reliability. Regarding the perception on the SQFs, the significant difference among the male and female customers has been noticed in the perception on reliability, responsiveness and tangibles.

All SERVQUAL scale on all SQFs among the male and female customers are in negative. It shows that the customers are not satisfied upto their level of expectation. Higher deviation among the male and female customers is identified in assurance and empathy. Regarding the SERVQUAL scale, the significant difference among the male and female customers has been identified in the case of reliability, responsiveness and assurance. Both the male and female customers are moderately satisfied towards the banks.

The significantly and positively influencing SQFs on the customers' satisfaction among the male customers are reliability and responsiveness, whereas among the female customers, these are responsiveness, assurance, tangibles and empathy. The higher discriminate power is identified in the case of responsiveness and empathy. Regarding the perception on SQFs, the important discriminate SQFs among the male and female customers is responsiveness and it is identified as higher among female customers.

The highly perceived SQFs among the less educated customers are responsiveness and reliability whereas among the educated customers, these are empathy and responsiveness. Among the highly educated customers, these are reliability and empathy. Regarding the level of perception on SQFs, the significant difference among the three educated groups of customers are reliability and empathy. The SERVQUAL scale on SQFs among the customers is negative. The higher negative SERVQUAL scale is identified in empathy among the less educated customers whereas among the educated and highly educated customers, it is identified in assurance and reliability. Regarding the SERVQUAL scale on SQFs, the significant difference among the three educated customers has been noticed in the case of reliability, responsiveness.

Regarding customers' satisfaction towards banking, the less educated customers are highly satisfied than the highly educated customers. The significantly and positively influencing SQFs on customers' satisfaction among the less educated customers are responsiveness and assurance whereas among the educated customers, these are reliability, responsiveness and empathy. Among the highly educated customers, these SQFs are reliability, responsiveness, assurance and empathy. Regarding the perception on SQFs, the higher discriminate power is identified in the case of empathy and reliability. The important discriminate SQFs among the different educated groups of customers are empathy and reliability and these are higher among highly educated customers than less educated customers.

By the income of the customers, they are classified into Less Income Groups (LIGs) Middle Income Groups (MIGs) and High Income Groups (HIGs). The highly perceived SQFs among LIGs are tangibles and empathy whereas among the MIGs, these are tangibles and reliability. Among the HIGs, the highly perceived SQFs are responsiveness and empathy. Regarding the perception on SQFs, the significant difference among the three income groups of customers has been noticed in the case of reliability, responsiveness, assurance and empathy.

The negative SERVQUAL scale on all SQFs among all income groups of customers reveals that the customers are not satisfied upto their level of expectation on SQFs. Among the LIGs, the higher SERVQUAL scale is noticed in the case of assurance whereas among the MIG and HIGs, it is identified in empathy and tangibles. Regarding the SERVQUAL scale, the significant difference among the three income groups has been noticed in the case of tangibles and empathy.

Regarding customer satisfaction towards banks, the customers are moderately satisfied. The significantly and positively influencing SQFs on customer satisfaction among the LIGs are reliability and empathy whereas among the MIg, these are reliability, responsiveness and empathy. Among the HIG, these SQFs are reliability, responsiveness, assurance, tangibles and empathy. The higher discriminate power to discriminate the three income groups of customers is identified in the case of empathy and reliability. The important discriminate factor among the three income groups of customers are empathy and reliability.

The highly perceived SQFs among the convenience seekers are empathy and tangibles whereas among the performance seekers, these are empathy and responsiveness. Regarding the perception on SQFs, the significant difference among the convenience and performance seekers has been identified in the perception on reliability, responsiveness, assurance and empathy.

All SERVQUAL scale on SQFs is negative. It indicates that the level of perception among the customers is less than their level of expectation on SQFs. The higher negative SERVQUAL scale among the convenience seekers is identified in the case of empathy whereas among the performance seekers, it is identified in 'assurance'. Regarding the SERVQUAL scale on SQFs, the significant difference among convenience and performance seekers has been noticed in the case of assurance and empathy.

Higher customer satisfaction towards the banks has been seen among the performance seekers than among the convenience seekers. The significantly and positively influencing SQFs on customer satisfaction among the convenience seekers are tangibles and empathy whereas among the performance seekers, these SQFs are reliability, responsiveness and assurance. The higher discriminate power of SQF is noticed in the case of assurance and reliability. The important higher discriminate SQFs among the convenience and performance seekers is identified in the case of reliability and responsiveness.

Based on occupation, the customers are classified into agriculturalists, employees and businessmen. The highly perceived SQFs among the agriculturalists are empathy and tangibles whereas among the employees, these are reliability and assurance. Among the businessmen, the highly perceived SQFs are responsiveness and reliability. The level of perception on SQFs among the businessman is greater than the level of perception among the other two groups of customers. Regarding the level of perception, the significant difference among the three groups of customers has been identified in their perception on reliability and responsiveness.

The SERVQUAL scale on all SQFs among the agriculturalists, employees and businessman is negative. It reveals that the customers are not satisfied utpo their level of expectation. Regarding the SERVQUAL scale on SQFs, the significant difference among the three groups of customers has been noticed in the case of reliability, responsiveness and empathy. The agriculturalists are more satisfied towards banks than the other two groups of customers.

The significantly and positively influencing the SQFs on the customer satisfaction among the agriculturalists are reliability and empathy. Among the employees, these SQFs are reliability, responsiveness and assurance whereas among the businessmen, these SQFs are reliability, responsiveness and empathy. The higher discriminate power is noticed in the case of reliability and responsiveness. The important discriminate SQFs among the three groups of customers are empathy and reliability.

Based on experience, the customers are classified into Less Experienced (LED), Experienced (ED) and Highly Experienced (HED). The highly perceived SQFs among the LED and ED, are empathy and reliability whereas among the less experienced, these are assurance and reliability. The less experienced customers rate the SQFs higher than the other groups of customers. Regarding the perception on SQFs, the significant difference among the three groups of customers has been identified in the case of reliability, responsiveness and empathy.

Among the Less Experienced customers, the positive SERVQUAL scale is identified in the case of reliability and empathy whereas among the experienced customers, it is noticed in empathy alone. In all other SQFs, the SERVQUAL scale is noticed to be in negative. Regarding the SERVQUAL scale, the significant difference among the three groups of customers has been identified in the case of all five SQFs. The highly experienced customers are less satisfied than the other two groups of customers.

The significantly and positively influencing SQFs among the less experienced customers are reliability, assurance, tangibles and empathy whereas among the experienced customers, these SQFs are reliability, assurance and empathy. Among the highly experienced customers, the significantly and positively influencing SQFs are reliability, responsiveness and empathy. Higher discriminate power is noticed in the case of reliability and empathy. The important discriminate SQFs among the three groups of customers are reliability and tangibles. The less experienced customers show high perception on reliability and tangibles than the other two groups of customers.

Research Implications

The findings of the service quality in commercial banks replicate the findings of Mustag (2005)[1]; Kwan and Lee (1994)[2] and; Sharma and Jothi (2007)[3]. The important service quality factors in commercial banks are reliability, responsiveness, assurance, tangibles and empathy. The customers in New Private Sector Banks have relatively higher expectation and perception on service quality compared to the customers in Private Sector and Public Sector banks. But all customers in all three groups of banks are not satisfied upto their level of expectation. The gap between the level of perception and expectation is very high in Public Sector Banks. This findings confirms the previous findings (Elango and Gudep, 2006[4]; Joshua and Moli, 2005[5]). The important discriminate SQF perception among the three groups of customers are found in empathy and assurance.

The demographic profile of the customers play an important role in the customers' expectation on the service quality factors. The service quality is highly expected by the urban customers than the rural customers. The important discriminate service quality factors are reliability and empathy. These findings are the extension of the previous research findings (Lassar et al., 2000[6]; Srivastava 1994[7]; and Bhat, 2005[8]). Age is also a significant discriminator for the service quality expectations especially on reliability, responsiveness and assurance. The above said service quality factors are highly expected by the youngster than the elders. These results recall the findings of Hansman and Schutjens (1993)[9] and; Easingwood and Storey (1993)[10].

An interesting finding for gender is that the female customers are expecting more service quality. than the male customers. The important discriminate service quality expectations among them are empathy and reliability. The findings reveals that the marketing strategies emphasizing service quality may be more effective for women than for men. This finding is just contractory to the findings of the previous studies (Gani and Mushtag, 2003[11]; Anthony and Adams, 2000[12]; Jun et al., 1999[13]). The higher income group of customers are expecting more service quality than the lower income groups. The important discriminate service quality expectations among the lower, middle and higher income groups of customers are reliability and responsiveness. It might be because the higher income customers may be attached with higher runover at banks and they may have more knowledge on banking facilities and service qualities offered in the banking industry. This finding reflects the findings of Ugur et al., (1997)[14]; Christopher Jones (2003)[15] and Zeithmal et al., 1990[16]). The performance seekers show high expectation on reliability, responsiveness and assurance whereas the convenience seekers expect more on empathy and tangibles. The important discriminate SQFs among the convenience and performance seekers are reliability and responsiveness which is also indicated by Gordon (1994)[17], Parasuraman et al., (1991)[18] and Hood and Walters (1985)[19].

Occupation is also an important discriminator of the service quality expectations among the customers. The businessmen are expecting more service quality than the employees and agriculturalist. The empathy and reliability are the important discriminate service quality factors among them. These findings have been already noted by Lewis (1991)[20] and; Coskun and Fronhlich (1992)[21]. The experienced customers expect more service quality than the less experienced customers. The important discriminate service quality factors among the three levels of experienced customers are assurance and responsiveness which replicates the findings of Sachdev and Verma, 2002[22]; Kenmeth, 1994; and Lianxi Zhut, 2004[23]).

The customer segmentation analysis, has revealed that the urban customers are perceiving more on SQFs than the rural customers. The service quality gap among the urban and rural customers are in negative. It reveals that these customers are not satisfied upto their level of expectation. The service quality factors have a significant and positive impact on customer satisfaction. The important discriminate service quality perception among the urban and rural customers is found in reliability, responsiveness and empathy. These results reflect the findings of Teas and Wong, 1991[24]; Thwaites and vere, 1995[25]).

Age is the one of important discriminators of the perception on service quality of commercial banks. The aged customers perceive more on service quality factors than the other two age groups of customers. Among all age groups, the customers' perception on SQFs is not upto the level of their expectation. The aged customers are highly satisfied towards banks than the other two age groups. The significantly influencing perception on SQFs on the customer satisfaction among the aged customers is higher in the case of reliability, responsiveness, tangibles and empathy. The important discriminate service quality perception among the three age groups of customers is found in empathy and tangibles which support the findings of Laroche and Taylor, 1988[26]; Anderson et al., 1993[27]).

The gender based analysis has been made on the perception on SQFs. It revealed that both male and female customers are not satisfied upto their level of expectation even though the female customers are more satisfied towards SQFs than the male customers. The maximum number of four SQFs have a significant and positive impact on customer satisfaction among the female customers. The important discriminator service quality perception among the male and female customers is responsiveness. The findings of the study support the views of Sripes et al., (2006)[28]and Amin (1994)[29].

The educational qualification of the customer is discriminated by their perception on empathy and reliability. The highly educated customers are highly satisfied than their counterparts. The significantly influencing SQFs on the customer satisfaction is identified as higher among the highly educated than the less educated. These findings prove the segmentation difference in the perception on SQFs among the customers which is also mentioned by Zeithaml et al., (1996)[30], How Gaft (1991)[31] and Natarajan et al., (1999)[32].

The income of the customers is one of important discriminators of service quality perception among the customers. Even though, all income groups are perceiving less on SQFs compared to their level of expectation, the higher income groups perceive more than the other income groups. It indicates that the service quality of commercial banks is mainly focused on the higher income groups. The important discriminators of the service quality perception among the three groups of customers are empathy and reliability which has been mentioned by Lassar et al., (2000)[33] and Verma and Hema (2001)[34].

The performance seekers are completely different from the convenience seekers regarding their perception on SQFs. The important discriminate SQFs among them are reliability and responsiveness. The significantly influencing SQFs on customer satisfaction among the convenience and performance seekers are completely different. These results indicate the differentiated strategies to fulfill the needs of the two groups of customers, which also suggested by Jamal and Nassan, 2002[35]; Jun and Cai, 2001[36]; and Mam and Sahmi 2008[37]).

The analysis of the occupation of the customers reveals that, the service quality gap is higher among the businessmen because of their higher and ever changing expectations. The significantly influencing SQFs on their satisfaction towards the banks are also different among the three groups of customers. The important discriminate SQFs among the three groups are empathy and reliability. This is frequently identified by the previous studies (Sharma and Mehta, 2005[38]; Aggarwal and Gupta, 2003[39]).

The highly experienced customers are more sensitive on the perception on SQFs compared to the other two groups. The significantly influencing SQFs on customer satisfaction among the less experienced are more than that among the highly experienced customers. The changes in perception on SQFs explain that the changes in their satisfaction towards banking is higher among the less experienced customers. The important discriminate service quality perception among the three groups are found in reliability and tangibles. It reveals the need for different approaches to satisfy different groups of customers which has already been revealed by Roberts et al., (2003)[40].

Managerial Implications and Recommendations

The data analysis provides some interesting insight into customers' expectation and perception on service quality factors in commercial banks. Based on the findings of the study, the following managerial implications are drawn.

Regarding the service quality expectations, the demographic profile of the customers namely, age, gender, level of education, income, nativity, occupation and years of experience are playing an important role. The level of expectations of each SQF among the different groups of customers, under each profile, differ from each other. The bank managers are advised to study the profile of their customers and their level of expectation on SQFs, before framing any marketing strategy. Only then they can generate the effective marketing strategy for each segment of the customers.

For example, the urban and rural customers are not unique in their level of expectation on SQFs. What is highly required by the urban customers may not be highly expected by the rural customers. Similarly the level of expectation on SQFs among male customers is different from female customers. Since the competition in banking industry is hectic, the bank managers should find their own appropriate marketing strategy according to the nature of their customers and environment. A proper training should be given to the managers to analyse the strength, weakness, opportunity and threat to their banks.

Even in the same bank, the different marketing strategies are essential to satisfy the different groups of customers. Because of the versatile nature of the customers, their level of expectation and requirements may differ. The bank managers should try to design and deliver personalized banking service to their customers. Hence, the shift from "customerised service" to personalized services is highly essential to satisfy all groups of customers.

The bank managers in general, may also find the results useful. Many services are primarily employee-driven businesses, requiring high levels of employee/customer partipartion. For such businesses, result of this study suggests that perceived levels of service quality importance vary between different groups in each demographic variable. More specifically, these service providers might realize that a move toward mechanization, similar to ATMs and Tellers usuage, may not be lucrative if their market is geared toward older adults, and that the variety and availability of services are more meaningful to women. These same services might also want to spotlight the reliability and honesty of their employees, particularly if the business deals with an individual's personal possession.

The banks should focus on providing training and support systems that enable service providers to offer error-free transactions. The institutions might consider positioning their banks as the one who 'gets it right'. The convenience segment can be addressed, through the delivery system with express lanes at the banks and strategic placement of ATMs. New customers could be attracted to a bank through marketing programmes, that promote the bank's ability to deliver superior performance relative to competition. The key is to deliver that superior performance, a task that may require substantial training for bank personnel. Attracting new customers from the convenience segment, is an opportunity for those banks that have an extensive location and ATM network.

Since income is also one of the important discriminators of service quality expectation and perception on SQFs, the bank manager should carefully analyse the different income groups of customers and estimate their level of expectation on SQFs. Only then they can supply the right service to the right consumers. Even though, the services and service quality are superior compared to others, if these are not properly positioned among the right customers at the right time, the efforts taken by the managers will be in vain. Hence, the bank managers have to be very careful in analyzing the requirements of the various groups of customers, and only then, they can position the right product to the right customer at the right time.

Concluding Remarks

Based on the important measures that reflected the outcome and process dimensions, this research has identified two discriminate findings. At first, the study concludes that the profile variables of the customers have its own influence on the level of expectation on service quality factors. The analysis reveals the perception on the service quality factors among the different customer segments and the difference between the level of perception and expectation on service quality factors. The analysis on the level of expectation on service quality factors, reveals that the profile of the customers play an important role in the determination and discrimination of the service quality expectations. Regarding the perception on service quality factors, the significant differences among the different groups of customers based on their profile have been identified. The perception on service quality factors is not upto the level of expectation on service quality factors among customers segment. But the degree of deviation between the level of perception and expectation depends upon the profile of the customers. This study suggests the importance of demographic profiles of the customers, before introducing the new service/service quality to the customers. The findings of the study stresses upon the importance of placing right service quality to the right customers at right time. It is the mantra for the success of commercial banking in the globalised era.

REFERENCES

1. Mushtag A.Bhat (2005), "Correlatives of Service Quality in Banks: An Empirical Investigation", *Journal of Service Research,* 5(1), April-September, pp. 77-98.

2. Kwan, W and Lee, T.J (1994), "Measuring Service Quality in Singapore Retail banking", *Singapore Management Review*, 6(4), pp. 7-11.

3. Sharma, R.D and Jyothi Sharma (2007), "Measurement of Consumer Delight in Indian Banking", *GITAM Journal of Management*, 5(2), pp. 130-142.

4. Rengasamy Elango and Vijayakumar Gudep (2006), "A Comparative Study on the Service Quality and Customer Satisfaction Among Private, Public and Foreign Banks", *The ICFAI Journal of Marketing Management*, 5(3), pp. 8-23.

5. Joshua A.J and Moli. P. Koshi (2005), "Expectations and Perceptions of Service Quality in Old and New Generation Banks – A study of select Banks in the South Canara Region", *Indian Journal of Marketing*, 39(9), September, pp. 6-11.

6. Lassar, W.M., Manolis, C and Winsov, R.D (2000), "Service Quality Perspectives and Satisfaction in Private Banking", *Journal of Services Marketing*, 14(2&3), pp. 244-272.

7. Srivastava, A.K (1994), "Customer Service in Banks: Need for a Marketing Approach", in Bidhi, C (1994), *Marketing of Services* (Ed.) New Delhi, Rawat Publication, pp. 25-38.

8. Mushtag A Bhat (2005), "Service Quality Perceptions in Banks: A Comparative Analysis", *Vision*, 9(1), January-March, pp. 11-20.

9. Hansman, H and Schutjens, V (1993), "Dynamics in Market Segmentation: A Demographic Perspective on Age-specific Consumption", *Marketing and Research Today*, 21(3), pp. 139-147.

10. Easingwood, C.J and Storey, C.D (1993), "Market Place Success Factors for New Financial Services", *Journal of Services Marketing*, 7(1), pp. 41-54.

11. Gani, A and Mushtag B.A (2003), "Service Quality in Commercial Banks: A Comparative Study", *Paradigm*, 7(1), pp. 24-36.

12. Anthony, T.A and Adams, H.C (2000), "Service Quality at Banks and Credit Unions: What do their customer say?", *Managing Service Quality*, 10(1), pp. 52-60.

13. Jun, M., Peterson, R.J., Zsidision, G.A and Daily, B.F (1999), "Service Quality Perceptions in the Banking Industry: Major Dimensions", *Journal of Business Strategies*, 16(2), pp. 170-188.

14. Ugur Yavas, Donald. J. Shemwell and Zeynep Bilgin (1997), "Service Quality in the Banking Sector in an Emerging Economy: A Consumer Survey", *International Journal of Bank Marketing*, June, pp. 217-223.

15. Christopher Jones (2003), "Quality and Productivity in Arab Banking", *Management Services*, Enfield, 47(1), January, p. 8.

16. Zeithmal, V.A Parasuraman, A., and Berry, L.L (1990): "Delivering Quality Service Balancing Customer Perceptions and Expectations". *The Free-Press*, New York.

17. Gordon, HG. Mc. Dougall and Terrence J.Levesqm (1994), "Benefit Segmentation using Service, Quality Dimensions an Investigation in Retail Banking", *International Journal of Bank Marketing*, 12(2), pp. 15-23.

18. Parasuraman, A., Berry, L.L and Zeithaml, V.A (1991), "Understanding Consumer Expectation of Service", *Sloan Management Review*, Spring, pp. 39-48.

19. Hood, J.M and Walters, C.G (1985), "Banking on Established Customers", Journal of Retail Banking, 4(4), pp. 8-13.

20. Lewis, B.R (1991), "Service Quality: An International Comparison of Bank Customers' Expectations and Perceptions", *Journal of Marketing Management*, 7(1), pp. 47-62.

21. Coskun, A., Fronhlich, C.J (1992), "Service: The Competitive Edge in Banking", *Journal of Services Marketing*, Vol. 6, pp. 15-22.

22. Sheetal B.Sachdev and Hansh V.Verma (2002), "Customer Expectation and Service Quality Dimensions Consistency", *Journal of Management Research*, 2(1), April, pp. 43-52.

23. Lianxi Zhut (2004), "A Dimension–specific Analysis of Performance only Measurement of Service Quality and Satisfaction in China's Retail Banking", *Journal of Services Marketing*, 18(7), pp. 534-546.

24. Teas, R.K and Wong, J (1991), "Measurement of Customer Perceptions of the Retail Bank Service Delivery System", *Journal of Marketing Management*, 7 (1), pp. 147-167.

25. Thwaites, D and Vere, L (1995), "Bank Selection Criteria – A Student Perspective", *Journal of Marketing Management*, 11(2), pp. 133-149.

26. Laroche, M., and Taylor, T (1988), "An Empirical Study of Major Segmentation Issues in Retail Banking", *International Journal of Bank Marketing*, 6(1), pp. 31-48.

27. Anderson, E.A and Sullivan, M.W (1993), "The Antecedents and Consequences of Customer Satisfaction for Firms", *Marketing Science*, 12(1), pp. 125-143.

28. Robin L.Sripes and F.Thomson and Sharon L.Oswald (2006), "Gender Bias in Customer Evaluations of Service Quality: An Empirical Investigation", *Journal of Services Marketing*, 20(4), pp. 274-284.

29. Amin, M.E (1994), "Gender As a Discriminating Factor in the Evaluation of Teaching", *Assessment and Evaluation in Higher Education*, 19(2), pp.135-143.

30. Zeithaml, V.A, Parasuraman, A and Berry, L.L (1996), "The Behavioural Consequences of Service Quality", *Journal of Marketing,* April, 00.31-46.

31. HowGaft, J.B (1991), "Customer Satisfaction in Retail Banking", *Service Industry Journal,* January, pp. 11-17.

32. Angur, M.G., Natarajan, R and Jahera, J.S (1999), "Service Quality in the Banking Industry: An Assessment in a Developing Economy", *International Bank Marketing,* 17(3), pp. 116-123.

33. Lassar, M, C.Manolis and Winson, D (2000), "Service Quality Perspectives and Satisfaction in Private Banking", *Journal of Services Marketing,* 14(2&3), pp. 244.

34. Verma, D.P.S and Hema, I (2001), "Market Orientation in Commercial Banks: A Study of Selected Banks in Delhi", *Vision,* July-December, pp. 7-14.

35. Jamal, A and Naser, K (2002), "Customer Satisfaction and Retail Banking: An Assessment of some of the Key Antecedents of Customer Satisfaction in Retail Banking", *International Journal of Bank Marketing,* 20(4), pp. 146-61.

36. Jun, M and Cai, S (2001), "The Key Determinants of Internet Banking Service Quality: A Content Analysis", *International Journal of Bank Marketing,* 19(7), pp. 276-296.

37. Mann, B.S and Sunpreet Sahin(2008), "Understanding Customer Service Quality and Customer Loyalty of Internet Banking in Private and Public Sector Banks", *Gyan Management,* 2(1), Jan-June, pp. 129-140.

38. Alka Sharma and Versha Mehta (2005), "Service Quality Perceptions in Financial Services – A Case Study of Banking Services", *Journal of Services Research,* 4(2), October-March, pp. 205-221.

39. Navadeep Aggarwal and Mohit Gupta (2003), "Multi Level–Multi Dimentional Model of Banking Service Quality", *Paradigm,* 8 (2), July-December, pp. 91-104.

40. Roberts, K., Varki, S and Brodie, R (2003), "Consumer Services: An Empirical Study in Banking", European Journal of Marketing, 37(1-2), pp. 169-196.

Bibliography

BOOKS

Crossby, P.B., (1979), *Quality is Free: The Art of Making Quality Certain,* McGraw Hill, New York.

Dangar Research Group Limited (1991), *Quality Service Study,* April-May.

Edvardsson, B., Thomasson, B and Ovretveit, J (1994), *Quality of Service.* Barrie Dale, London.

Kotler, P and Armstrong, G (1991), *Principles of Marketing,* 5th ed., Prentice-Hall, Eaglewood cliffs, NJ.

Oliver, R.L (1997), *A Behavioural Perspective on the Consumer,* McGraw-Hill, New York.

Rust, R.T and Oliver, R.L (1994), "Service Quality: Insights and Managerial Implications from the Frontier", *Service Quality: New Directions in Theory and Practice,* Sage Publications, Thousand Oaks, CA.

Smith, A.M., (1992), The Consumers' Evaluation of Service Quality: Some Methodological Issues in Glynon, W.J., and Barnes, J.P., (1995) *Understanding Service Management,* (eds.) New York, John Wiley and Sons.

Srivastava, A.K (1994), "Customer Service in Banks: Need for a Marketing Approach", in Bidhi, C (1994), *Marketing of Services* (Ed.) New Delhi, Rawat Publication.

Zeithaml, V.A and Bitner, M.J (2000), *Services Marketing: Integrating Customer Focus across the Firm,* McGraw Hill, Newyork, NY.

Zeithaml, V.A., Parasuraman, A., Berry, L.C., (1990), *Delivering Quality Services: Balancing Customer Perception and Expectations,* New York, Free Press.

JOURNALS

Abdulah H. Aladdaigan and Francis A-Buttle (2002), "Systra – SQ: A New Measure of Bank Service Quality", *International Journal of Service Industry Management,* 13(4).

Agarwal, M.C. and Suhud S. Bapat (2000), "Impulse Buying in Services: Status and Research Directions", *Developing Service Quality,* M.Raghavachari and K.V.Ramani, Mc Millan India Ltd., Delhi.

Ahire, S.L., Golhar, D.Y. and Waller, M.A (1996), "Development and Validation of TQM Implementation Constructs", *Decision Sciences,* 27(1).

Ajaya Kumar Mohanty (2005), "Customers Service in Banks: An Overview", *Professional Banker,* 5 (1), January.

Albrecht, K., and Zemke, R., (1985), "Service America: Doing Business in the New York in Lewis, Bartara, (1991), "Service Quality: An International Comparison of Bank Customers Expectation and Perceptives", *Journal of Marketing Management,* 7(1).

Alka Sharma and Versha Mehta (2005), "Service Quality Perceptions in Financial Services A Case Study of Banking Services", *Journal of Services Research,* 4(2), October-March.

Alok Mittal, Jayant Sonwalkar and Akhilesh K.Mishra, (2003), "An Exploratory Study of CRM Orientation Among Bank Employees", *Indian Journal of Training and Development*, 33 (1-2), January-June.

Amit Mokerjee and G.Shainesh (2000), "Developing Measures for Service Quality and Relationship Strength Determinants of Customers Loyalty", *Developing Service Quality*, M. Raghavachari and K.V.Ramani, Mcmillan India Ltd., Delhi.

Ammannaya, K.K (2004), "Indian Banking: 2004", *IBA Bulletin*, 26(1), January.

Andaleeb, SS and Basu, A.K. (1994), "Technical Complexity and Consumer Knowledge As Moderators of Service Quality Evaluation in the Automobile Service Industry", *Journal of Retailing*, 20(4).

Anders Gustafsson and Michael D.Johnson (2004), "Determining Attribute Importance in a Service Satisfaction Model", *Journal of Services Research*, 7 (2), November.

Anderson, E.A and Sullivan, M.W (1993), "The Antecedents and Consequences of Customer Satisfaction for Firms", *Marketing Science*, 12(1).

Anderson, J.C and Gerbing (1988), "Structural Equation Modeling in Practice — A Review and Recommended Two-step Approach", *Psychological Bulletin*, 103(3).

Anderson, W.T., Cox, X.P., III and Fulcher, D.H. (1976), "Bank Selection Decisions and Market Segmentation", *Journal of Marketing*, 40(1).

Angur, M.G., Natarajan, R. and Jahera, J.S., (1999), "Service Quality in the Banking Industry: An Assessment in a Developing Economy", *International Journal of Bank Marketing*, 17 (3).

Anthony, T.A and Adams, H.C (2000), "Service Quality at Banks and Credit Unions: What do Their Customer Say?", *Managing Service Quality,* 10(1).

Aravindan, P. and Punniyamoorthy, (2000), "Service Quality Model to Measure Customer Satisfaction", *Delivering Service Quality,* M.Raghavachari and K.V.Ramani, Mc Millan India Ltd.

Babakus, E and Inhofe, M (1991), "The Role of Expectations and Attribute Importance in the Measurement of Service Quality", in Gilly Mc. (ed). Proceedings of the Summer Educator's Conference, Chicago, IC: *American Marketing Association.*

Babin, B.J., and Boles, J.S., (1998), "Customer Behaviour in a Service Environment: A Model and Test of Potential Difference Between Men and Women", *Journal of Marketing,* 62 (April).

Balakus, E and Boller, G.W. (1992), "An Empirical Assessment of the Servqual Scale", *Journal of Business Research,* 24(3).

Bendapudi Neeli and Leonard L. Berry (1997), "Customers Motivation for Maintaining Relationships with Service Providers", *Journal of Retailing,* 73 (1).

Bernett, D., and Higgins, M., (1988), "Quality Means More Than Smiles", *ABA Banking Journal,* June.

Berry, L.C. and Parasuraman, A., (1997), "Listening to the Customers–The Concept of A Service Quality Information System", *Gloan Management Review,* Spring.

Bharati Pathak (2003), "A Comparison of the Financial Performance of Private Sector Banks", *Finance India,* 17 (4), December.

Bolton, R.N., and Drew, J.H. (1991), "A Multistage Model of Customer's Assessment of Service Quality and Value", *Journal of Consumer Research,* 17(4).

Bowen, J.W. and Hedges, R.B., (1993), "Increasing Service Quality in Retail Banking", *Journal of Retail Banking,* 15 (1).

Brady Micahel and Cronin, Joseph, J., (2001), "Some New Thoughts on Conceptualizing Perceived Service Quality: A Hierarchical Approach", *Journal of Marketing,* 65 (3).

Brady, M.K. Cronin, J and Brand, R.R (2002), "Performance only Measurement of Service Quality: A Replication and Extension", *Journal of Business Research,* 5(1).

Brown, S.W., Chruchill, G.A. and Beter, J.P. (1993), "Improving the Measurement of Service Quality", *Journal of Retailing,* 69(1).

Burnelt, J.J. and Wilkes, R.E., (1985), "An Appraisal of the Senior Citizens Market Segment", *Journal of Retail Banking,* 7(4).

Burnelt, J.J., Chonko, L.B., (1984), "A Segmental Approach to Packing Bank Products", *Journal of Retail Banking,* 6(2).

Carman, J.M., (1990), "Consumer Perceptions of Service Quality: An Assessment of the SERVQUAL Dimensions", *Journal of Retailing,* 66(1).

Chinedu B Ezirim (2005), "Empirical Investigation of Customer's Choice of Retail Banks in Nigeria", *The ICPAI Journal of Applied Economics,* 4 (5), September.

Chowdhary, Nunit and Bhagawati P.Saraswat (2004), "Service Leadership Study", *Journal of Services Research,* 3 (2).

Christopher Jones (2003), "Quality and productivity in Arab Banking", *Management Services,* Enfield, 47(1), January.

Churchill, G.A, Jr (1979), "A Paradigm for developing better measures of marketing constructs", *Journal of Marketing* 16 (February).

Clement (2005), "Service Quality Gap Models: A Re-examination and Extension", *SMART Journal of Business Management Studies,* 1 (2), July-December.

Coskun, A., Fronhlich, C.J (1992), "Service: the Competitive Edge in Banking", **Journal of Services Marketing**, Vol. 6.

Cronin, J.J., Brady, M.K and Hult, T.M. (2000), "Assessing the Effects of Quality, Value and Customer Satisfaction on Consumer Behavioural Intentions in Service Environments", *Journal of Retailing,* 76(2).

Cronin, J.J. and Taylor, S.A. (1992), "Measuring Service Quality: A re-examination and Extension", ***Journal of Marketing,*** 56 (3).

Darshan Parikh, (2002), "Measuring Retail Service Quality: An Empirical Study in a Developing Country", *South Indian Journal of Management,* 12 (2), April-June.

Debasish Sathya Swaroop (2003), "Service Quality in Commercial Banks: A Comparative Analysis of Selected Banks in Delhi", *Indian Journal of Marketing,* 33 (3).

Deborah F.Spake, Sharon E.Beathy, Beverly K. Brockman and Tammy Neal Crutchfield (2003), "Consumer Comfort in Service Relationships", *Journal of Services Research,* 5 (4).

Devlin, S.J. and Dong, H.K., (1996), "Service Quality from Customers Perspective", *Marketing Research,* 6 (1).

Dobholhar, P.A., Shepherd, Dc and Thorpe, D.I (2000), "A Comprehensive Framework for Service Quality: An Investigation of Critical, Conceptual and Measurement Issues Through a Longitudurial Study", *Journal of Retailing,* 76(2).

Donthu, N and Yoo. B (1998), "Cultural Influence on Service Quality Expectations", *Journal of Service Research,* 1(2).

Easingwood, C.J and Storey, C.D (1993), "Market Place Success Factors for New Financial Services", *Journal of Services Marketing,* 7(1).

Eminbabakus, Ugur Yavas and Osman, Karatepe (2003), "The Effect of Management Commitment to Service Quality on Employees' Affective and Performance Outcomes", *Journal of the Academy of Marketing Science,* 31 (3).

Fornell, G and Lancher, D.M (1981), "Evaluating Structural Equation Modeling with Unobservable Variables and Measurement Error", *Journal of Marketing Research,* 18(1).

Gagliamo, Kathryn, B., and Jan Hathcote (1994), "Customer Expectations and Perceptions of Service Quality in Retail Appraisal Specialty Stress", *Journal of Service Marketing,* 8(1).

Gagliano, K.B. and Itathcote, J., (1994), "Customer Expectation and Perceptions of Service Quality in Retail Apparel Speciality Stores", *Journal of Services Marketing,* 8(1).

Gani, A. and Mushtag, A. Bhat (2003), "Service Quality in Commercial Banks: A Comparative Study", *Paradigm,* 7 (1).

Gordon, HG. Mc. Dougall and Terrence J.Levesqm (1994), "Benefit Segmentation Using Service, Quality Dimensions – An Investigation in Retail Banking", *International Journal of Bank Marketing,* 12(2).

Greenfield, T.K and Altkisson, C.C (1989), "Steps Towards a Multifactorial Satisfaction Scale for Primary Care and Mental Health", *Evaluation and Programme Planning,* 12(3).

Gwin, J.M., Lindgren, J.H., (1982), "Banking on Established Customer", *Journal of Retail Banking,* 4(4)

Haider Yasmeen and M.V. Supriya (2008), "Organisational Role Stress: Confirmatory Factor Analysis approach", *Asia-Pacific Business Review,* 4(2), April-June.

Hansman, H and Schutjens, V (1993), "Dynamics in Market Segmentation: A Demographic Perspective on Age-specific Consumption", *Marketing and Research Today,* 21(3).

Hasanbanu, S., (2004), "Customer Service in Rural Banks: An Analytical Study of Attitude of Difficult Type of Customers Towards Banking Services", *IBA Bulletin,* 25 (8), August.

Hasmukh D.Savlani (2000), "Delivering Quality Services at Two Commercial Co-operative Banks in Gujarat", *Delivering Service Quality,* M. Raghavachari and K.V. Ramani, Mc Millan India Ltd..

Heilman, M.E., Martell, R.F. and Simon, M.C., (1989), "The Vagaries of Sex Bias: Conditions Regulating the Undervaluation, Equivaluation and Overvaluation of Female Job Applicants", *Organ Behaviour and Human Decision Proc.,* Vol. 41.

Henderson, R.I., (1984), *Performance Appraisal,* Reston Publishing Co., Reston, VA.

Hood, J.M and Walters, C.G (1985), "Banking on Established Customers", *Journal of Retail Banking,* 4(4).

Hood, J.M., and Walkers, C.G., (1985), "Banking on Established Customers", *Journal of Retail Banking,* 7(1).

HowGaft, J.B (1991), "Customer Satisfaction in Retail Banking", *Service Industry Journal,* January.

Israel, D., Celement Sudhahar and M.Selvam, (2004), *"Journal of Indian Management",* 1 (4), October-December.

Jamal, A and Naser, K (2002), "Customer Satisfaction and Retail Banking: An Assessment of some of the Key Antecedents of Customer Satisfaction in Retail Banking", *International Journal of Bank Marketing,* 20(4).

Joseph, M., McClure, C. and Joseph, B., (1999), "Service Quality in the Banking Sector: The Impact of Technology on Service Delivery", *International Journal of Bank Marketing.*

Joshuva, A.J. and Moli, P. Koshi (2005), "Expectations and Perceptions of Service Quality in Old and New

Generation Banks-A Study of Selected Banks in the South Canara Region", *Indian Journal of Marketing,* 35 (9), September.

Jun, M and Cai, S (2001), "The Key Determinants of Internet Banking Service Quality: A Content Analysis", *International Journal of Bank Marketing,* 19(7).

Jun, M., Peterson, R.J., Zsidision, G.A and Daily, B.F (1999), "Service Quality Perceptions in the Banking Industry: Major Dimensions", *Journal of Business Strategies.*

Juran, J., (1968), *Juran on Planning for Quality, American Society for Quality Control,* Milwankee, WI.

Kamilia Bahia and Jacques Nantel (2000), "A reliable and valid measurement scale for the Perceived Service Quality of Banks", *International Journal of Bank Marketing.*

Kassim, N.M. and Bojei, J (2002), "Service Quality: Gaps in Telemarketing Industry", *Journal of Business Research,* 55(11).

Kassim, N.M. and Bojei, J., (2002), "Service Quality: Gaps in the Telemarketing Industry", *Journal of Business Research,* 55 (11).

Kinnaird, D., Shaughnessy, K., Struman, K.D., Sinnyar, W.R., (1984), "Market segmentation of Retail Bank Services: A model for Management", *Journal of Retail Banking,* 6(3).

Krishnaveni, R. and Divya Prabha, (2005), "Service quality and its linkages with customer relationship management-A comprehensive view", *Udyog Pragati,* 29 (3), July-September.

Kwan, W and Lee, T.J (1994), "Measuring Service Quality in Singapore Retail banking", *Singapore Management Review.*

Laroche, M., and Taylor, T (1988), "An Empirical Study of Major Segmentation Issues in Retail Banking", *International Journal of Bank Marketing,* 6(1).

Lassar, M, C.Manolis and Winson, D (2000), "Service Quality Perspectives and Satisfaction in Private Banking", *Journal of Services Marketing,* 14(2&3).

Lassar, W.M., Manolis, C and Winsov, R.D (2000), "Service Quality Perspectives and Satisfaction in Private Banking", *Journal of Services Marketing,* 14(2&3).

Lawche, M. and Taylor, T., (1988), "An Empirical Study of Major Segmentation Issues in Retail Banking", *International Journal of Bank Marketing,* 6(1).

Lenis, B., (1991), "Service Quality: An International Companion of Bank Customers Expectations and Perceptions", *Journal of Marketing Management,* 7 (1).

Levist, T (1981), "Marketing Intangible Products and Product Intangibles", *Harvard Business Review,* 59(3).

Lewis, B.R (1991), "Service Quality: An International Comparison of Bank Customers' Expectations and Perceptions", *Journal of Marketing Management,* 7(1).

Lewis, B.R., Orledge, J and Mitchell, V.W (1994), "Service Quality: Students Assessment of Banks and Building Societies", *International Journal of Bank Marketing,* 12(4).

Lewis, P.E. (2001), "An Extension to the Process of Customer Service Quality Evaluation Through Psychology and Empirical Study", *Asia-Pacific Advances in Consumer Research.*

Lianxi Zhut (2004), A dimension–specific Analysis of Performance only Measurement of Service Quality and Satisfaction in China's Retail Banking", *Journal of Services Marketing* 18(7).

Line Lervik Olsen and Michael D. Johnson (2003), "Service Quality, Satisfaction and Loyalty: Transaction-Specific to Cumulative Evaluations", *Journal of Service Research,* 5 (3), February.

Lovelock, C.H (1983), "Classifying Services to Gain Strategic Marketing Insights", *Journal of Marketing,* 47(3).

Mackie, D., Hamilton, D., Susskind, J., and Rosselli, F., (1996), "Social Psychological Foundations of Stereotype Formation", in Macrae, C.N., Stangor, C. and Hewstone, M., (Eds.), *Stereotypes and Stereotyping,* The Guilford Press, New York, NY.

Madhu Vij (2003), "The New World of Banking", *Journal of Management Research,* 3 (3), December.

Mann, B.S and Sunpreet Sahin(2008), "Understanding Customer Service Quality and Customer Loyalty of Internet Banking in Private and Public Sector Banks", *Gyan Management,* 2(1), Jan-June.

Milind Sathye (2005), "Privatisation, Performance and Efficiency: A Study of Indian Banks", *Vikalpa,* 30 (1), January-March.

Mushtag A Bhat (2005), "Service Quality Perceptions in Banks; A Comparative Analysis", *Vision,* 9(1), January-March.

Mushtag A. Bhat (2005), "Correlates of Service Quality in Banks: An Empirical Investigation", *Journal of Services Research,* 5 (1), April-September.

Mushtag A.Bhat (2005), "Correlates of Service Quality in Banks: An Empirical Investigation", *Journal of Services Research,* 5(1), April-September.

Mushtag A.Bhat (2005), "Service Quality Perceptions in Banks; A Comparative Analysis", *Vision - The Journal of Business Perspectives,* 9(1), January-March.

Narasimhan, C. and Sen, S. (1992), "Measuring Quality Perceptions", *Marketing Letters,* 3 (1).

Navadeep Aggarwal and Mohit Gupta (2003), "Multi Level–Multi Dimentional Model of Banking Service Quality", *Paradigm,* 8 (2), July-December.

Navdeep Aggarwal and Mohit Gupta (2003), "Multi Level-Multi Dimensional Model of Banking Service Quality", *Paradigm,* 7 (2), July-December.

Nazrul Islam and Ezaz Ahmed, (2005), "A Measurement of Customers Service Quality of Banks in Dhaka City of Bangladesh", *South Asian Journal of Management,* 12 (3).

Nergron-relazemey, G; Alegnia, M; Vera, M and Freeman, D.H (1998), "Testing the Service Satisfaction Scale in Puerto Rico", *Evaluation and Programme Planning,* 21(1).

Niki Glaveli, Eugenia Petridon, Chris Liassides and charalambos Spathus (2006), "Bank Service Quality: Evidence from Five Balkan Countries", *Managing Service Quality,* 16(4).

Olive Nerurkar (2000), "A Preliminary Investigation of SERVQUAL Dimensions in India", *Delivering Service Quality:* M.Raghavachari and K.V.Ramani, Mc Millan India Ltd.

Oliver, R.L. (1981), "Measurement and Evaluation of Satisfaction Process in Retail settings?, *Journal of Retailing,* 57 (6).

Oliver, R.L., (1980), "A Cognitive Model of the Antecedents and Consequences of Satisfaction Decisions", *Journal of Marketing Research,* 17 (3).

Oliver, R.L., (1993), "A Conceptual Model of Service Quality and Service Satisfaction: Compatible Goals, Different Concepts. In T.A. Swartz, D.E. Bowen and S.W.Brown (eds)., Advances in Services Marketing and Management: Research and Practice, Greenwich, CT:JAI, Vol. 2.

Olsen, S.O (2002), "Comparative Evaluation and the Relationship Between Quality, Satisfaction and Repurchase Loyalty", *Journal of the Academy of Marketing Sciences,* 30(3).

Parasuraman, A., Berry, L.L and Zeithaml, V.A (1991), "Understanding Consumer Expectation of Service", *Sloan Management Review*, Spring.

Parasuraman, A., Zeithaml, V and Berry, L (1988), "SERVQUAL: a Multiple Item Scale for Measuring Consumer Perceptions of Service Quality", *Journal of Retailing Spring* (64).

Parasuraman, A., Zeithaml, V and Berry, L. (1985), "A Conceptional Model of Service Quality and Implications for Future Research", *Journal of Marketing,* Fall (49).

Parasuraman, A., Zeithaml, V.A., (1988), "SERVQUAL: A Multiple Item Scale for Measuring Consumer Perceptions of Service Quality", *Journal of Retailing,* 64 (1).

Parasuraman, A., Zeithaml, V.A., and Beny, L.L., (1994), Alternative Scales of Measuring Service Quality: A Comparative Assessment based on Psychometric and Diagnostic Criteria", *Journal of Retailing,* 70 (3).

Parasuraman, A., Zeithaml, V.A., and Berry, L., (1985), "A Conceptual Model of Service Quality and its Implications for Future Research", *Journal of Marketing,* 49 (Fall).

Patterson, P.G and Spreng, R.A (1997), "Modelling the Relationship Between Perceived Value, Satisfaction and Repurchase Intention in a Business-to-Business, Services Context: An Empirical Examination", *International Journal of Service Industry Management,* 8(5).

Peter, J.P., Chruchill, G.A and Brown, T.J. (1993), "Caution in the Use of Different Scores in Consumer Research", *Journal of Consumer Research,* 19 (March).

Plank, R.E., Greene, R.C. and Greene, J.N (1994), "Understanding which Spouse Makes Financial Decisions", *Journal of Retail Banking,* 16(1).

Powell, T.C., (1995), "Total Quality Management as Competitive Advantage: A Review and Empirical Study", *Strategic Management Journal,* 16 (1).

Prabhakaran, S., and Satya, S., (2003), "An Right into Service Attributes in Banking Sector", *Journal Services Research,* X 3(1), April-September.

Prithviraj Nath and Arinvandan Mukherjee (2000), "Measuring Service Quality in Engineering Education-Applicability of SERVQUAL", *Delivering Service Quality,* M.Raghavachari and K.V.Ramani, Mc Millan India Ltd.

Ramasamy (1996), "Design and Management of Service Process: Keeping Customers for Life", Addison-Wesley, Reading MA.

Raptnaja Gogula and Roli Sehgal (2004), "Service communication challenges in the tourism Industry: Gap 4 of De Integrated Gaps Model of Service Quality Revisited through selected cases", *The ICFAI Journal of Marketing Management,* November.

Rawani, A.M. and Gupta, M.P. (2000), "It Vs Service Quality in Banks-A Few Learning Issues", *Delivering Service Quality,* M. Raghavachari and K.V.Ramani, Mc Millan India Ltd.

Rengasamy Elango and Vijayakumar Gudep (2006), "A Comparative Study on the Service Quality and Customer Satisfaction among private, public and foreign banks", *The ICFAI Journal of Marketing Management,* 5(3).

Robert Johnston (1997), "Identifying the Critical Determinants of Service Quality in Retail Banking: Importance and Effect", *International Journal of Bank Marketing;* 15(4).

Roberts, K., Varki, S and Brodie, R (2003), "Consumer Services: An Empirical Study in Banking", *European Journal of Marketing,* 37(1-2).

Robin L.Sripes and F.Thomson and Sharon L.Oswald (2006), "Gender bias in Customer Evaluations of Service Quality: An Empirical Investigation", *Journal of Services Marketing,* 20(4).

Ronald L. Hess, Shankar Ganesan and Naveen M.Klerin, (2003), "Service Failure and Recovery: The Impact of Relationship Factors on Customer Satisfaction", *Journal of Academy of Marketing Science,* 31 (2).

Ruyter, K.D. and Bloemer, J. (1995), "Integrating Service Quality and Satisfaction: Playing in the Neck or Marketing Opportunity?", *Journal of Customer Satisfaction, Dissatisfaction and Complaining Behaviour,* 8 (2).

Sanjai K Jain and Garima Gupta (2004), "Measuring Service Quality" SERVQUAL Variables SERVPERF Scales", *Vikalpa,* 29(2), April-June.

Sanjay Kumar, (1999), "Profitability of Indian Commercial Banks-The Key Discriminators", *Management and Accounting Research,* 1 (4), April-June.

Sanjay, K. Jain and Garima Gupta, (2004), "Measuring Service Quality: SERVQUAL Variables SERVPERF scales", *Vikalpa,* 29(2), April-June.

Shainesh, G. and Mukul Mathur, (2000), "Service Quality Measurement: The Case of Railway Freight Services", *Vikalpa,* 25 (3), July-September.

Shajahan, S., (2000), "A Study on the Level of Customers Satisfaction on Various Models of Banking Services in India", *The ICFAI Journal of Bank Management,* 4(1), February.

Sharma, R.D and Jyothi Sharma (2007), "Measurement of Consumer Delight in Indian Banking", *GITAM Journal of Management,* 5(2).

Sheetal B. Sachdev and Harsh V. Verma (2002), "Customer Expectations and Service Quality Dimensions Consistency", *Journal of Management Research,* 2 (1), April.

Sheetal B. Sachdev and Harsh V. Verma, (2004), "Relative Importance of Service Quality Dimensions: A Multi Sectoral Study", *Journal of Services Research,* 4 (1), April-September.

Sheetal B.Sachdev and Hansh V.Verma (2002), "Customer Expectation and Service Quality Dimensions Consistency", *Journal of Management Research,* 2(1), April.

Shemwell, D.J; Yavas, U and Bilgin, Z (1998), "Customer-Service Provider Relationships: An Empirical Test of a Model of Service Quality, Satisfaction and Relationship-oriented Outcomes", *Internatinal Journal of Service Industry Management,* 9(2).

Shid Mahmood (2001), "Customer Quality in Education: An Exploratory Study", *Management and Change,* 5 (2), Winter.

Sivaloganathan, K., (2004), "Relationship Marketing in Banking Service: The Need of the Hour", *Udyog Pragati,* 28 (2), April-June.

Speed, R. and Smith, G., (1992), "Retail Financial Services Segmentation", *The Service Industrial Journal,* 12(3).

Sultan Singh (2004), "An Appraisal of Customers Service of Public Sector Banks", *IBA Bulletin,* 25 (8), August.

Sundar, K. and Lakshmanan (2005), "Customer Care Management in Banks", *Management Marketers,* 1 (3), September-February.

Sundaram, S., (1984), "Customer Service in Banks at Cross Roads", *The Journal of the Indian Institute of Bankers,* 55 (4).

Takeuchi, H and Quelch J.A (1983), "Quality is more than making a Good Product", *Harvard Business Review,* July-August.

Teas, K.R (1993), "Expectation, Performance Evaluation, and Consumer's Perceptions on Quality", *Journal of Marketing,* 57 (October).

Teas, R.K and Wong, J (1991), "Measurement of Customer Perceptions of the Retail Bank Service Delivery System", *Journal of Marketing Management*, 7 (1).

Thompson, A.M and Kaminski, P (1993), "Psychographic and Lifestyle Antecedents of Service Quality Expectations: A Segmentation Approach", *Journal of Services Marketing*, 7(4).

Thwaites, D and Vere, L (1995), "Bank Selection Criteria – A Student Perspective", *Journal of Marketing Management*, 11(2).

Ugur Yavas, Donald. J. Shemwell and Zeynep Bilgin (1997), "Service Quality in the Banking Sector in An Emerging Economy: A Consumer Survey", *International Journal of Bank Marketing*, June.

Upinder Dhar, Santosh Dhar and Abhinav Jain, (2004), "Service with a Difference: A Comparative Analysis of Private and Public Sector Banks", *Prestige Journal of Management and Research*, 8 (1 & 2), April-October.

Verma, D.P.S and Hema, I (2001), "Market Orientation in Commercial Banks: A Study of Selected Banks in Delhi", *Vision*, July-December.

Verma, D.P.S. and Hema Israney, (2001), "Market Orientation in Commercial banks–A Study of Selected Banks in Delhi", *Vision*, 6 (1), July-December.

Verma, D.P.S. and Ruchika Vohra, (2000), "Customer Perception of Banking Service Quality–A Study of State Bank of India", *The Journal of Institute of Public Enterprise*, 23 (3 & 4).

Victor Iglesias (2004), "Pre-conceptions about Service", *Journal of Service Research*, 7 (1), August.

Wallaied M. Lassar and Robert D. Winsor (2000), "Service Quality Perspectives and Satisfaction in Private Banking", *Journal of Services Marketing*, 14 (2-3).

Webster, C. (1989), "Can Consumers be Segmented on the Basis of Their Service Quality Expectations?", *Journal of Service Marketing,* 3 (2).

Westbrook, R.A and Oliver, R.L (1991), "The Dimensionality of Consumption Emotion Patterns and Consumer Satisfaction", *Journal of Consumer Research,* 18(1).

Withowski, T.H. and Wolfinbarger, M.F. (2002), "Comparative Service Quality: German and Americal Rating Across Service Settings", *Journal of Business Research,* 55(11).

Xavier, M.J. and Shainesh, G., (2000), "Modelling Customer Evaluation of Banking Service–The Antecedents and Consequences of Service Value", *Delivering Service Quality,* M. Raghavachari and K.V.Ramani, Mc Millan India Ltd., Delhi.

Yogeshwari Phatak and Naseem Abidi (2000), "Client's Perception on Quality in Banking Services: An Empirical Study", *Delivering Service Quality,* M. Raghavachari and K.V.Ramani, Mc Millan India Ltd.

Zeithaml, V.A (1988), "Consumer Perceptions of Price, Quality, and Value: A Means End Model and Synthesis of Evidence", *Journal of Marketing,* Vol. 52, July.

Zeithaml, V.A, Parasuraman, A and Berry, L.L (1996), "The Behavioural Consequences of Service Quality", *Journal of Marketing,* April.

Zeithaml, V.A. Berry, L.L and Parasuraman, A (1993), "The Nature and Determinants of Customer Expectations of Service", *Journal of the Academy of Marketing Science,* 21(1), Winter.

Zillur Rahman (2005), "Service Quality: Gaps in the Indian Banking Industry", *The ICFAI Journal of Marketing Management,* February.

Index